An Introduction to
Spoken Interaction

Learning About Language

General Editors:
Geoffrey Leech and Mick Short,
Lancaster University

An Introduction to Spoken Interaction

Anna–Brita Stenström

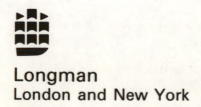

Longman
London and New York

Longman Group UK Limited,
Longman House, Burnt Mill,
Harlow, Essex CM20 2JE, England
and Associated Companies throughout the world.

*Published in the United States of America
by Longman Publishing, New York*

© Longman Group UK Limited 1994

First published 1994

ISBN: 0–582 07130–5 PPR

British Library Cataloguing-in-Publication Data
A catalogue record for this book is available from the British Library

Library of Congress Cataloging in Publication Data
Stenström, Anna-Brita, 1932–
    An introduction to spoken interaction / Anna-Brita Stenström.
        p.   cm. — (Learning about language)
    Includes bibliographical references and index.
    ISBN 0–582–07130–5
    1. Oral communication.   2. Discourse analysis.   I. Title.
    II. Series.
    P95.S76   1994
    302.2'242—dc20   93–26729
                                                                CIP

Set in 11/12pt Bembo by 8U
Printed in Malaysia by TCP

Contents

Key to symbols

Prosodic symbols

#	tone unit boundary
\	fall
/	rise
=	level
\\/	fall-rise
/\	rise-fall
\ /	fall + rise
/ \	rise + fall
.	brief silent pause
–	unit silent pause
– –(–)	longer than unit
ə(m)	brief voiced pause (often spelt *uh, um*)
ə:(m)	long voiced pause (often spelt *er, erm*)
★ ★	overlapping speech
{ }	subordinate tone unit
| |	enclosing phonetic symbols (eg |ð|)
(( ))	enclosing subaudible elements

♣♣♣ Words spelt with capital letters carry nucleus

Other symbols

☆	backchannelling
>	current speaker continues
. . .	more is said
[ ]	move
< >	act
S	Subject
P	Predicator
O	Object
C	Complement
A	Adverbial
I	Initiate
R	Response
F	Follow-up
♣♣♣	Nota bene
▶▶▶▶▶	Exercise

♣♣♣ (A, B, C) indicate surreptitious speakers;
small letters (a, b c) indicate non-surreptitious speakers (whose speech has not been prosodically transcribed);
(1.3:35–48) etc refers to text and tone units in the London-Lund Corpus.

Preface

What is spoken interaction?

When we are talking to each other we are not just pronouncing words. By saying something we are also doing something; an interrogative utterance such as *Did you lock the front door?* can, for instance, function as a request for information or a reproach or a warning, depending on the circumstances. When we say something we also expect the addressee to respond in one way or another; by answering a question, by agreeing (or disagreeing) to a proposal, by acknowledging receipt of information, and so on, in other words by being an active partner. This is what spoken interaction is about.

Spoken interaction belongs to the area of discourse, which can be defined as 'any unit of language beyond the sentence', such as a dialogue in speech and a paragraph in writing. Discourse is either spoken or written. The main difference between the two is that spoken discourse chunks information into **tone units** marked off by tone unit boundaries (with or without pauses), while written discourse chunks information into clauses and sentences marked off by punctuation marks.

This book deals only with spoken, interactive discourse produced by two speakers (dialogues) or more than two speakers (multilogues). It describes various types of face-to-face and telephone interaction.

Why study spoken interaction?

So far we know much more about the rules and principles that govern the written language than about those governing the spoken language. But we all use the spoken language to interact with each other, and generally to a much greater extent than we use the written language, so it is highly important that we know how spoken interaction is structurally and strategically organized. Also, the same or similar principles are valid for a large number of languages, so studying the organization of spoken interaction in one language helps us understand the interactional principles of other languages.

What, then, is spoken interaction like? That is the question this book will try to answer.

What this description is based on

The description is based on naturally occurring spoken interaction, as manifested in the London-Lund Corpus of English conversation (described in Svartvik and Quirk 1980, Svartvik (ed.) 1990). The London-Lund Corpus consists of tape-recordings covering approximately half a million words, which have been orthographically transcribed with a detailed prosodic analysis in terms of tone units, intonation, pauses, etc. (following Crystal 1969), and ultimately computerized. The speakers are adult, educated British English speakers, some of whom know each other well ('intimate') and some not ('distant').

Genuine extracts from the corpus will be used as illustrations, but in order to facilitate reading, the prosodic marking has been reduced to the bare minimum (tone unit boundaries, intonation contours and pauses). Slips of the tongue and double brackets indicating subaudible speech have occasionally been omitted, if they do not illustrate a particular point. The speakers are generally referred to as A and B, in that order, regardless of what they are called in the original (lower case letters indicate non-surreptitious speakers).

The model of analysis that I am going to introduce is partly a modification of the model introduced for classroom interaction by Sinclair and Coulthard (1975), partly an adaptation of conventions adopted by other discourse and conversation analysts and partly my own invention. Due to the unpredictability of natural conversation, the model may not be a hundred per cent reliable. On the other hand, it can certainly be applied to languages other than English. What makes it particularly useful is its openness to changes when the need arises. The book as a whole draws on many sources and can be seen as a synthesis of much of the work that has been done so far in the analysis of conversation.

How this book is organized

The aim of this book is to show how spoken interaction in general and, ultimately, different types of spoken interaction are structurally and strategically organized.

Chapter 1 presents an overview of what is typical of spoken interaction in general. The idea is that this overview should prepare the reader for what is coming in subsequent chapters. Chapter 2 presents the five-level model of analysis, further developed in Chapter 3, which constitutes a detailed description of the main strategies speakers use in conversation. Chapter 4 goes from a description of the structure of conversation in general to a comparison of different types of conversation. In Chapter 5, finally, there is a brief discussion of the link between spoken interaction and grammar.

How to use this book

The book is meant to be used as a textbook, section by section, and the reader is strongly advised to do the exercises accompanying each section to get a good grasp of the analysis. For those already familiar with this type of analysis, the book can of course be used as a reference book.

At the end of each chapter you will find a list of book titles. These are books that I found helpful and that you are advised to read if you want to go deeper into a particular problem. A few recently published books have been added.

Acknowledgements

What made it at all possible to write the book was first, the availability of a large corpus of recorded and transcribed conversation, the London-Lund Corpus of Spoken English, second, the permission of Malcolm Coulthard and John Sinclair to use their model for analysing classroom interaction as a point of departure for a more comprehensive discourse model, and third, the authorization of Sidney Greenbaum to listen to the tape-recordings at the Survey of English Usage, University College London.

I am most grateful to Jan Svartvik for encouraging remarks on the first chapter of the book and to Karin Aijmer, Angela Hasselgren, and especially Vibecke Haslerud for reading and commenting on the whole manuscript. My thanks also to students at Stockholm University and Bergen University for not complaining when being exposed to preliminary chapters of the book.

CHAPTER 1
General characteristics

What is typical of spoken interaction?

Spoken interaction is a joint, here-and-now social activity which is governed by two main principles:

- speakers take turns
- speakers cooperate

When studying transcripts of genuine conversation one is struck by the general atmosphere of cooperativeness and harmony. This does not mean, of course, that the listener always waits for the speaker to finish before taking over. Nor does it mean that speakers never disagree, object, or contradict each other. Moreover, interaction is possible without proper turntaking, namely in cases where there is (temporarily) a dominant speaker and the other party's contribution is reduced to so-called 'backchannels' (realized by items like *m, yes, oh, I see, really*) as a sign of attention.

A small set of lexical items, such as *well, sort of*, and *you know*, have a positive impact on the smooth flow of conversation. They help the speaker to take, keep and yield the turn and to appeal for feedback.

Since spontaneous speech is delivered on the spot, speaker turns usually contain various types of hesitation phenomena, such as silent and filled pauses (marked . – ə:m in the transcriptions; see Key to symbols), verbal fillers (*well, I mean, sort of*), false starts, repetitions, and incomplete utterances. Therefore, the grammar is often fairly intricate, while the vocabulary, especially in everyday conversation, tends to be very general and not much varied.

It is no exaggeration to say that questions and answers constitute the backbone of conversation. Questions can be used to start a conversation and they can be used over and over again to keep it going and rekindle it when it is on the point of fading out. In narrative parts of a conversation, on the other hand, informs, ie speech acts which offer information, play the main role. The role of questions is illustrated in extract [1], the role of informs, together with most of the linguistic features that characterize spoken interaction, in extract [2]. Prosody has been omitted, with the exception of brief and unit pauses (. and –; see p 7). The asterisks indicate simultaneous speech.

Two examples

Two young university secretaries are discussing study prospects:

		[TURNS]
[1] A:	**isn't it going to be a strange and impossible task for me picking up linguistics** and I'm entirely . at least almost entirely ignorant of it at present .	1
B:	go to find out the right seminars to go to that's what I did when I first came	2
A:	the right seminars . yes .	3
B:	you know I went to some .	4
A:	cos *lectures are rather a waste of* time are they	5
B:	*what did you read English* or not	6
A:	yes I read English but only from Kyd onwards so that you see I didn't even do any Old English or any Anglo-Saxon at all .	7
B:	**I don't suppose you need Old English and Anglo-Saxon**	8
A:	well no . but əm you know *I don't have any language*	9
B:	*əm well I hadn't* done any English at all you know since O-level .	10
A:	yea .	11
B:	and I went to some second year seminars where there are only about half a dozen people *and* they discussed what a	12
A:	*m*	☆

B: word was *and − * what's a sentence
A: *m* ☆
B: that's *ev*en more difficult .
A: *yeah* yeah − ☆
B: and so on . . . (1.5:1–43)

'Questioning sequences' are used in three places, the first beginning in turn 1, the second in turn 6, and the third in turn 8. The primary role of the questions is of course to elicit an answer; doing so, they also keep the conversation going. The reason why turn 5 (*cos *lectures are rather a waste* of time are they*) does not receive an answer is probably that it is simultaneous with turn 6. B simply ignores it. The minimal response items *m*, *m*, and *yeah* yeah are all backchannels (indicated by ☆) which let B go on speaking. They are consequently not turns.

An instance of partly overlapping speech is found in turns 9 and 10, where A says *I don't have any language* at the same time as B says *əm well I hadn't*. Hesitation markers are represented by *but əm you know* in turn 9 and *əm well* in turn 10. In addition, *you know* has a 'social' function, appealing for understanding.

Extract [2] is part of a narrative, where a young girl, A, is telling a female friend, B, about her recent holidays in Spain. She is apparently very excited. This is not so much reflected in her actual words as in her search for words:

[TURNS]

[2] A: . . . but it's so nice and relaxed down 1
there **I mean** compared with London −
I mean I I I . I found myself − going
into shops and people smiled at you and **I**
. I was quite taken aback genuinely **I ***
mean I *
B: *m* . m − . ☆
A: ə you know the feeling **you you you**
you you
B: yes *one asks oneself if you're putting on 2
this deadpan face you know*
A: *((several sylls))* yes 3
B: yes 4
A: and these people smile and you − well 5
you don't know how to react at first
because it's so *strange*
B: *yes* I felt that 6

in Scotland – yes (– laughs)
(2.7:1277–92)

Notice the multiple repetitions of *I*, and *you* in turn 1, and the two attempts at reformulations starting by *I mean* in turn 1 (*I mean I I, I *mean I**). Like *you know*, *I mean* appeals for understanding and sympathy, and it is a useful device for adding an afterthought (turn 1). *Well* in turn 5 seems to have a similar function. The fact that A cannot wait for B to finish is reflected in the inaudible speech, indicated by '((several sylls))' in turn 3.

Speakers take turns

Turns

A **turn** is everything the current speaker says before the next speaker takes over. Some turns are very short and consist of a single word, like turns 1 and 4 in the following telephone closing:

		[TURNS]
[3] B:	right	1
A:	yes thanks very much	2
B:	OK bye	3
A:	bye	4

Other turns are very long and resemble short monologues, as in the extract below (dealing with the 'Irish question'):

[4] TURN
A: but I don't **I mean** . because. because in Ireland . everyone insists on remembering things right back to – əm Henry the second – **I mean** all those things are important this is where the British . **just sort of** completely can't understand them because . **I mean** all we're we're quaintly interested in – things that happened . two hundred years ago here **I mean** they are of historical . interest – but it doesn't really affect our day to day thinking – but . **I mean** . I don't . **I mean** ...
(2.8:280–89)

And A continues. Notice the extensive use of **verbal fillers**, especially *I mean*, which indicates that the speaker is busy planning what to say as he goes along. Notice also that there are two main hesitation areas, at the beginning of the turn (*but I don't*

I mean . because . because) and what looks like the end but is really the middle of the turn (– *but . I mean . I don't . I mean*).

Speaker shifts

In the ideal case, speakers wait for each other to stop talking before starting to speak. The result is a **smooth speaker shift**. But if one party takes over without waiting for the other to stop talking, the result is an **unsmooth speaker shift** where part of what one speaker says overlaps with part of what the other says, or s/he is simply **cut off**.

Speaker shifts	
SMOOTH	B lets A finish before taking the turn and vice versa
UNSMOOTH	B does not let A finish before taking the turn and vice versa
CUT-OFF	A stops short when B starts to speak and vice versa

Consider the following extract later in the dialogue about the Irish question:

> [5] B: I mean – – – the British are at a loss in a sense to
> understand problems like this because it doesn't fit –
> it doesn't fit into any of the criteria – that . əːm –
> they understand being I mean sort of *rather a
> ((dull lot of . . .))*
> A: *well I just feel you know personally I think you
> all* well know my feelings about this I just . feel that
> the whole business about partition was terribly
> terribly unjust (2.8:323-35)

Speaker B has apparently lost the thread, as indicated by the verbal fillers (*I mean, sort of, rather*). A, on the other hand, is eager to present his opinion and simply butts in. At this point, the takeover is fairly simple.

Backchannels

Not all utterances are proper turns. **Backchannels** are not. What distinguishes backchannels from turns is that they do not involve a speaker shift. On the contrary, they acknowledge what the current speaker says and generally encourage her/him to go on.

But since they are inserted in the course of the current talk, they
often cause partial overlaps (> in the transcriptions indicates that
the same speaker goes on):

> [6] A: well look if in that case I'd like to do it . I mean I
>   really want to do *it* I'm not being
>   B: *yes*
>   >A: funny *or anything*
>   B: *no no* (3.1:494–500)

B's *yes*, overlapping with A's *it*, expresses agreement with *I really
want to*, and B's *no no*, which overlaps with B's *or anything*
expresses agreement with *I'm not being funny or anything*.

The listener, of course, pays more attention to the message
than to the syntax, with the result that backchannels often
interfere with the syntactic continuity of the utterance. Such
interferences are generally overlooked by the current speaker:

> [7] A: . . . I just felt you know
>   B: *yes yes quite yes*
>   >A: *I didn't want to be* pressurized like that any
>   more (3.2:470–74)

However, backchannels are perhaps more often inserted at
syntactic and semantic 'completion points', where even a
takeover would have been natural:

> [8] A: it really makes me sick I mean I refused to go to
>   university point blank because the only subject I
>   wanted to do was French
>   B: m
>   >A: and I felt that I wouldn't . do what was required of
>   me in French anyway (1.5:1002–08)

Verbal feedback may of course be replaced by silent
feedback in the form of gestures, head nods, eye glances, and
facial expressions. Another, very frequent feedback signal is
laughter.

What is done in a turn?

What we say in a turn may start a conversation, it may keep it
going or terminate it. By saying something we make the other
party respond in one way or the other – or there would be no
conversation. For example, a question requires an answer, to

mention the obvious case. Moreover, whatever we say means something, and it means something 'in that particular context'. In other words, the turn is part of the structural organization of the conversation, and what is said is part of the interactional and pragmatic strategies adopted by the speaker to make the listener understand what s/he intends.

However, the string of words produced can have more than one meaning: the **literal** (word-by-word) meaning, the **intended** meaning (what the speaker intends), and the **perceived** meaning (what the listener understands). See further pp 25–6.

A turn is not just a continuous flow of speech

We write in sentences, but do we also speak in sentences? Not really. Do we speak in clauses? Well, that depends. What we can safely say, is that when we speak we divide the flow of words into some kind of units, whether they be pause units or tone units or a combination of both.

Pause units

Pauses reflect how we structure a message, where we hesitate, where we separate semantic-syntactic chunks and where we breathe. Roughly speaking, pauses can be said to mark off **performance units**, ie the strings of words that we manage to process in one go.

There are two types of pause, **silent** and **filled**. Both vary in length. The 'standard' length, **unit,** varies according to the rhythm of each individual speaker. In other words, pause length is relative.

---

silent pauses brief (.), unit (–), double (– –), treble (– – –)
filled pauses brief ∂m, unit ∂:m

Silent and filled pauses are used for partly the same, partly different purposes. Obviously, only silent pauses serve as **breathing** pauses; such pauses generally match semantic-syntactic boundaries. Both silent and filled pauses, often combined, are used for **hesitation** and for **strategic** purposes (eg taking, holding and yielding the turn), and to **mark off** units of discourse, eg topics and subtopics (pp 150–62).

Compare the combinations of silent and filled pauses below:

[9] **Hesitation pauses**
A: and what will it be .
B: əm – ə: an aperitival small whisky about that size .
(4.4:858–61)

[10] **Strategic pauses**
A: so that's the picture
B: ə:m – now this irons that I that I thought might be .
worth looking at if Carol . agreed . . . (2.6:1093–96)

In both cases, the pause combinations come at the beginning of a
turn. In the first case, what B says is a reaction to what A said; B
is offered a drink and cannot make up his mind right away. In the
second case, B starts talking about a new topic, using the pause as
a take-off. Some hesitation may of course be involved even here.

The problem with pause units is that hesitations are fairly
unpredictable. Speakers hesitate not only at the beginning of a
turn before making up their minds, but also in other places in the
turn. The pause unit is, therefore, not the ideal unit for describing
how we chunk an utterance.

Tone units

We speak with a certain rhythm, with the result that we
automatically divide utterances into word groups, or **tone units**.
The largest syntactic unit corresponding to a tone unit is generally
the clause (simple sentence). Moreover, the tone unit corresponds
directly to an **information unit** (see pp 9–10).

Each tone unit has one 'pitch-prominent' syllable carrying
the nuclear tone (the direction of which is marked by a little
arrow) and the main information load. Capital letters are used in
the transcription examples for the word containing the pitch-
prominent syllable. Tone units are marked off by tone unit
boundaries ('#'), which are often accompanied by a pause:

                                                          [TURNS]
[11] A: and D'YOU . teach# –   1
     B: NÒ# I DÓN'T# because I'm not   2
        ÈNGLISH at all#
     A: I SÈE# (1.5:457–61)   3

Turns 1 and 3 contain only one tone unit each. Turn 2 contains three tone units, the first consisting of one word (NO̖), the second of two words (I̖ DO̗N'T) and the third of six words (*because I'm not È̖NGLISH at all*). Notice that combinations of fall and rise are possible (eg I̖ DO̗N'T# in turn 2) and also that all the tone units, except NO̖# in turn 2, correspond to a clause.

Some turns contain so-called **subordinate** tone units (marked off by ({ }). The pitch range of such tone units falls within the pitch-range of the 'ordinary' tone unit, and is less prominent:

[12] A: you S=EE# we we . are members of the faculty of ÀRTS {**of the UNIVÉRSITY#**}# – (1.2:1377–78)

Complementary additions, afterthoughts and comments like *as you know* and *it seems to me*, and so on, tend to occur in a subordinate tone unit.

Tone units consist minimally of a **nucleus:** NO̖#

The maximal configuration is:

because I'm not È̖NGLISH at all#
(prehead) (head) NUCLEUS (tail)

Tone unit boundaries (#) mark the end of a tone unit

Subordinate tone unit boundaries ({ }) mark the beginning and end of subordinate tone units

Tones are: fall (\), rise (/), level (=), fall-rise (\/), rise-fall (/\), fall + rise (\ /), rise + fall (/ \)

The average length of a tone unit is four to five words but it can be as long as fifteen words or more. The length depends mainly on how fast the speaker talks; the faster s/he talks the larger the number of words per tone unit.

Tone unit length and the distribution of pitch-prominent syllables are related to the structure of information, as we shall see in the next section. The **pitch pattern**, or direction of tone, is related to speech function (cf p 25).

Information units

The prosodic division of turns into tone units is not completely arbitrary; it is a consequence of organization of information into **information units,** where the information focus is marked by

intonation, ie **nuclear tone**. In [13], each turn contains only one
tone unit and consequently only one information unit:

> [13] A: are you under the UNIVÈRSITY#
>   B: ÁM I#
>   A: under the UNIV=ERSITY# –
>   B: YÈS# (2.4:76–79)

In [14] the turn consists of three tone units, ie three
information units:

> [14] A: but I think . LÒNDON# is one of the FÈW places#
>   . where you have to create your ÒWN relaxation#
>   (1.8:621–23)

Exactly how a message is organized is up to the individual
speaker. It would, for instance, have been quite possible for A to
present the message in two information units if s/he had wanted
to focus on two instead of three items. Compare [14] with [15]
where the information is conveyed stepwise and the emphasis is
achieved not only through nuclear placement but also brief
pauses:

> [15] A: ... I was LÉFT# after . FÌNALS# – with the
>   impression that ((this)) is the sort of thing that
>   everybody **ATTÀINED**# . doing university
>   **FÌNALS**# – SÓMEHOW# . during the EXÀM# .
>   by some **MÌRACLE** or other# which it was for
>   MÈ# . that suddenly all this **STÙFF**# that they'd
>   whipped **THRÒUGH**# {in two WÈEKS#}# .
>   SÙDDENLY# . they were able to ÙSE# all this
>   **INFORMÀTION**# ŸOU know# almost in TÒTAL#
>   – – – (2.9:461–75)

Notice that the nuclear word, ie the information focus, is usually
at the end of the tone unit (according to the 'principle of end
focus').

Speakers talk about something

A conversation 'is about' something. This will be referred to as
the **message** of the conversation. The message is generally not
embarked upon at once, however, nor does the conversation end
abruptly as soon as the message has been dealt with.
    There is generally an **opening** where the parties greet each

other, ask about each other's health and maybe exchange a couple of polite phrases, and a **closing** where the parties 'settle the affairs' and say goodbye. The 'extra' warming-up and winding-up talk, which helps create a pleasant atmosphere and is particularly common in informal situations, is referred to as **phatic talk** (cf p 14):

> [16] A: I'm not – ÒH# THÀNKS# . not really
> CÒMFORTABLE# . like THÍS#
> B: M̂# – – – you got a CÓLD#
> A: – NÒ# . just a bit SNÌFFY# cos I'm – I ÀM
> CÓLD# and I'll be all right once I've warmed
> ÙP# – do I LÒOK as though I've got a CÓLD#
> ... (1.3:1–11)

Another type of talk that is embedded in the conversation without having anything to do with what is talked about is **speech-in-action**, for instance offering food or drink as in the following extract 1 where A gives an account of an oral exam that he has just been exposed to (see pp 161–2):

> [17] A: ... two papers in MÉDICINE# – one in
> THERAPÈUTICS# – one in SÙRGERY# one in
> OBSTÈTRICS# there are FÍVE# . but all of them
> have a multiple CHÒICE# as WÈLL# – S=O# –
> you KNÓW# there are FÍVE# plus multiple
> CHÒICE# . quite a . it covers quite a lot of
> GRǑUND actually# –
> b: I can imagine .
> A: Y=EAH# . and very GÈNERAL# as WÈLL# the
> QUÈSTIONS# EXTRÈMELY general# . I was
> QUÌTE surprised#
> b: **have some more wine** .
> A: M̂# S=O# you see it came to the VÍVA# ...
> (2.9:48–69)

Speaker b, who is a non-surreptitious speaker and whose speech has therefore not been prosodically analysed, offers wine: *have some more wine*. This is an example of speech-in-action, which should be distinguished from an **aside**. A typical aside would be, for instance, when a doctor and a nurse engaged in a conversation with a patient suddenly comment on some method of treatment between the two of them and then resume the conversation (see further p 161).

Opening, message, closing

Take, for instance, the following brief telephone conversation; a departmental secretary, A, calls a male academic, B:

[18] A: HELLÓ#

B: Mr HÙRD# it's professor CLÁRK's secretary# *from Paramilitary* CÒLLEGE# — **Opening**

A: *oh YÉS#*

professor Clark asked if you were . going to collect some SCRÌPTS {TONÌGHT#}# * SÒUND* scripts# .

B: *YÈS#* M̀HM#

A: if you'd collect them from Mr GÒRDON# *who will be going to* |ði:| PLÀ meeting# — **Message**

B: *Mr GÓRDON#* – YÈS# =M#

A: RÍGHT#

B: Y=ES#

* . thanks* very MÚCH#

A: *(– giggles)* OK̀# . B=YE# — **Closing**

B: B=YE#

(9.1:713–32)

Mr Hurd hears the signal, picks up the phone and answers *hello*. Professor Clark's secretary at the other end, introduces herself, addressing him by his name. A brief introduction makes way for a request, the real purpose of the call. The request is accepted, but to make sure that everything is in order, the secretary asks Mr Hurd to reconfirm the agreement (*RÍGHT – Y=ES*). The call is terminated by a thanking exchange (*thanks very MÚCH – OK̀*) and a farewell exchange (*B=YE – B=YE*).

Despite what may look like a mess there is a definite beginning and end and a purpose for the call. In other words, the telephone call consists of three main sections:

OPENING
MESSAGE
CLOSING

Not only does this example represent one of the standard formats of telephone calls, but the overall structure of face-to-face conversation can be described in very much the same way. We shall see more about this in Chapter 4.

The message

In some conversations the message consists of one single **topic**, in others of several different topics. Topics, in their turn, usually split up into **subtopics**.

Sometimes a topic is temporarily broken off by a **digression**, ie the introduction of a (completely) different topic, but much more common is the so-called **topic drift**, which is the result of an almost imperceptible shift from one related topic to the next.

In the following conversation, two colleagues, A and B, begin by talking about B's position before joining the department:

> [19a] A: where do YŎU come from# – – .
>   B: you mean where was I BEFŎRE# (1.6:1–2)

and he turns out to be a computer programmer:

> [19b] B: PRŎGRAMMING {COMPǓTERS#}# – THÀT'S
>   what Í do# (1.6:21–22)

This makes A think of a friend of hers who has a son working at the computer centre:

> [19c] A: YÈS# do you know Malcolm BŎWEN# over at
>   the COMPǓTER ÚNIT# (1.6:23–25)

They continue to talk about Malcolm:

> [19d] B: . . . and he took Sam and I back to his . to where
>   he was LĬVING# – and this was a FLÁT# now
>   where WÀS it# . . . (1.6:89–91)

After some time, the speakers return to the original topic:

> [19e] A: SŎ# – **there we** ÀRE# – do you LĬKE this work
>   HÉRE# . in this DEPÁRTMENT# (1.6:130–33)

The introduction, shifting and termination of topics and subtopics are sometimes signalled by **topic-boundary markers** (see e.g. p 173).

From an interactional point of view topics are dealt with in **transactions**, subtopics in **exchanges** or sequences of exchanges, ie the parts that make up a transaction. This will be dealt with in Chapter 2.

What speakers talk about hangs together

What makes a conversation hang together is first of all the interactional framework, which determines the overall conversational structure in terms of opening, message and closing. As we saw in the previous section, openings and closings are more or less purely interactive parts of a conversation, where not much is being talked about, while the topic of conversation belongs to the message section, which is not only interactively but also coherently and cohesively linked.

Coherence and cohesion

A discourse is said to be **coherent** if what the speakers say fits in and makes sense to the speakers in the actual context. Generally, coherent utterances are also **cohesively** linked, lexically, grammatically, prosodically, and interactionally, with the immediate discourse. As we shall see in the following extract, cohesive links can be either **overt** or **covert**. Two colleagues are discussing a somewhat controversial way of teaching:

LINES

[20] A: have you ever heard Professor MCCÀLL   1
LÉCTURE# – he's ((round)) at TÒPAS I   2
THÍNK#   3
B: *((NÓ#))*   4
A: *I* only ever went ÔNCE# . it was   5
ENÓUGH# –   6
B: M̌# – –   7
A: oh DÊAR# BRÎDGET will tell you THÁT#   8
she was at the same LÈCTURE#   9
B: M̌# – – what's he LÎKE#   10
A: oh he was TÊRRIBLE#   11
B: (– giggles)   12
A: TÈRRIBLE# – so ABSTRÚSE# – he does   13
SÒUND changes# and all THÁT# sort of   14
thing# you KNÓW#   15
B: (– – – laughs)   16

A: so ABSTRÚSE# he he you can't read his   17
writing on the BLÁCKBOARD# he uses a   18
BLÁCKBOARD# . and writes illegible   19
THÍNGS on it# *you KNÓW#* –   20
B: *M̀#*   21
A: which is a GRÈAT help# – and then he says   22
course if you don't UNDERSTÀND this# –   23
this subject's not for YÓU# . (. laughs) you   24
KNÓW#   25
B: (– laughs) – (1.6:894–923)   26

The number of arrows shows that the **lexical** and **grammatical** cohesive relationships are strong both within and between the turns, mainly in the form of **co–reference**, realized by:

* pronominal reference (eg *he* in lines 10, 11 etc referring back to *Professor MCCÀLL* and *THÀT* in line 8 referring to what A said in lines 4 and 5);
* lexical repetition (*LÉCTURE – LÈCTURE, ABSTRÚSE – ABSTRÚSE* and *BLÁCKBOARD – BLÁCKBOARD*);
* ellipsis (in lines 5 and 17, where 'there' and 'he was' can be inferred from the immediately preceding context.

In the first two cases (pronominal reference and lexical repetition) the cohesive links are overt; in the third case (ellipsis) they are covert. The reference is **anaphoric,** since what is being referred to has been mentioned earlier in the text. If it refers to something outside the context, as in line 23, where the pronoun *this* in *((if)) you don't UNDERSTÀND this*) refers to the situational context, ('what I am talking about') the reference is **exophoric**.

The most obvious example of **interactive** linking is realized by the question-response pairs in lines 1–4 and 10–11; another example is the *you KNÓW*-laughter sequences in lines 15–16 and 25–6. *M̀* in line 21, on the other hand, occurs at the same time as *you KNÓW* in line 20.

Prosodic linking is illustrated, for instance, in lines 1–4, where the rising pitch on *LÉCTURE* invites B to respond and the rise on the response *NÓ* encourages A to go on, which he does ending his utterance with a falling, completing, tone.

The absence of cohesive links does not prevent a conversation from being coherent, however. Conversational partners usually manage to interpret utterances as coherent by filling in the missing links, ie by making **inferences** on the basis

of the immediate context, previous experience, knowledge of the
world, and not least on the basis of the knowledge that they share
with the other speaker. Thus, if an utterance makes sense 'in that
particular situation', it is coherent, with or without cohesive
links. One example where inference can be observed is [21]:

> [21] A: have you got a PÉN# I'll leave a MÈSSAGE# .
>   (8:360–61)

There are no cohesive links, but the inference is that A wants to
borrow a pen in order to write the message.

Interactional signals and discourse markers

When we talk, we use certain very frequent items to start, carry
on, and terminate the conversation. Some of these items
constitute turns of their own or link turns together. These will be
referred to as **interactional signals**. Others are used as organizers
and turnholders within the turn, or as boundary markers. These
will be referred to as **discourse markers**:

> [22a] A: ... I SUPPÓSE# if you got experience in
>   American . university ADMINISTRÁTION# you
>   could still come BÀCK *here*
>   B: *m* ÒH yes# . CÈRTAINLY# **well** they're
>   desperate . for people to work in UNIVÉRSITIES#
>   cos the MÒNEY'S not good# *– so anyone*
>   A: *oh RÉALLY# . **well you know*** oh HÈRE#
>   {YÈAH#}# *M̀#*
>   B: *so* anybody who's soft enough to ENJÓY it# and
>   *sort*
>   A: *YÈS#*
>   >B: **of** *ac*tually want a JÒB# **you KNÓW#** is
>   *wel*comed with open
>   A: *YÈS#* *M̀#*
>   >B: ÀRMS# (1.5:1109–23)

All the items in bold belong to one of these categories. Without
them the dialogue would have looked as follows:

> [22b] A: ... if you got experience in American . university
>   ADMINISTRÁTION# you could still come BÀCK
>   here
>   B: they're desperate . for people to work in

UNIVÉRSITIES# cos the MÒNEY'S not good# –
so anyone
A: HÈRE#
C: so anybody who's soft enough to ENJÓY it# and
want a JÒB# is welcomed with open ÀRMS#
(1.5:1110–23)

What is left makes perfect sense, so has anything really got lost?
For one thing, the conversation is much less lively and less
'personal' without items signalling receipt of information,
agreement and involvement. And the complete absence of
simultaneous talk is not exactly characteristic of spontaneous
conversation.

One thing that the items used as interactional signals and
discourse markers have in common is that they can do more than
one thing in the discourse. Take for instance *oh*, which appears in
three different places. In the first place it reflects strong emphasis
and is equivalent in meaning to the following *CÈRTAINLY*; in
the second place it serves as a link between B's and A's turn, and
in the third place it serves as a link within the turn. Items of this
type will be dealt with in Chapter 2.

Adjacency pairs

Some turn sequences are pragmatically more closely linked than
others, with or without interactional signals. This is the case
when the first part of a pair acts as a stimulus for the second part
of the pair so that one cannot very well do without the other. If,
for instance, a question is not answered, it is either repeated or
the questioner gives up in much the same way as a telephone
summons either continues until you lift the receiver or dies away.
At the other end, there are cases where a response is not crucial
for the conversation to go on but where the absence of a response
would certainly be noticed. Imagine, for instance, that you tell a
person something noteworthy and that s/he does not bother to
respond. In the normal case, that would probably either make the
first speaker repeat what s/he said or comment on the fact that
the second speaker did not respond. Consider the following:

[23] A: time for TÉA# *would* you LÍKE some#
B: *YÈS#* YÈS# (1.4:7–10)

A missing response would certainly be noticed.
The most typical adjacency pairs are the following:

Adjacency pairs

apology	<----->	smoother
greeting	<----->	greeting
invitation	<----->	accept/decline
question	<----->	answer
request	<----->	accept/turn down

Conversation is teamwork

Conversation works smoothly only if A and B **cooperate**, and they have to do so on three levels: interaction, discourse organization, and communication. This means that they are expected to observe the basic rules for turntaking and to 'listen actively' when they are not speaking. They are also expected to transmit what they want to transmit in a way that does not cause misinterpretation, and be prepared to make inferences from the context, whenever that is required.

Speakers cooperate

According to the philosopher Grice (1975), conversation should work without problems if speakers follow the maxims which constitute his well-known **cooperative principle**:

Maxims

QUANTITY   make your contribution as informative as is required
QUALITY   do not say what you believe is false or that for which you lack adequate evidence
RELATION   be relevant
MANNER   be perspicuous, brief and orderly; avoid obscurity and ambiguity

---

If, on the other hand, one of the maxims is violated, the result is that the utterance acquires a new meaning in addition to the literal meaning. This new meaning, which can be inferred from the contextual situation, is referred to as **conversational implicature**. One example is [24]:

> [24] A: actually you'll probably get a CÁR won't you {as
> soon as you GÉT there#}#
> B: **can't DRÍVE#** (6.2:565–66)

B's response violates the relevance maxim and possibly the manner maxim. *can't DR$\widehat{I}VE$* is definitely not a direct answer to the question; it is neither 'yes' nor 'no'. B means what she says, but she also means something more. What she means without saying it is her **intended** implicature, which is likely to be 'probably not' (since I can't drive). In most cases A's intended implicature agrees with B's **perceived** implicature, ie B's interpretation.

Clearly, A can never be certain that B will interpret what s/he says in the way in which it was intended. But in a cooperative, especially face-to-face situation, this is not a serious problem. The fact that there is a misunderstanding will be obvious pretty soon and can be remedied on the spot.

Certain utterances are conventionalized expressions of, for instance, invitations, offers, and requests. There is no doubt what the speaker intends, although the form of the utterance does not necessarily reveal its function. The following is uttered during a tea break:

[25] A . . . have you got some M$\grave{I}$LK for M$\acute{E}$# (1.4:35)

It is certainly not intended to be taken as a *yes/no*-question but as a request.

Utterances of this type are sometimes called **conventional implicatures** (but generally known as 'conventionalized indirect speech acts').

Speakers say what is relevant

Besides Grice's cooperative principle, which seems to be an idealization of what really takes place in conversation, there is another principle that enables a smooth conversation, namely Sperber and Wilson's (1986) **principle of relevance**. According to this principle an utterance is 'relevant' if it fits the actual topical framework by adding something extra to the context and if it shows the speaker's intention. If so, 'the smallest possible processing effort' is required on the part of the hearer, and the reason for misunderstanding is minimal. Consequently, [25] would cause no problem whatsoever.

The principle of relevance would also explain why the play with words in the following extract makes sense to the parties involved but not necessarily to everybody else. Speaker A works as a part-time assistant to Peter, who supervises his PhD thesis. At this point in the dialogue A and B are discussing whether A should choose a different subject to be able to combine the work in the phonetics department with work on the thesis:

> [26] A: the thing to DÓ# is obviously to swing the PhD subject round to something – . nearer to what I'm being paid to DÓ# *you SÉE#*
> B: *so you've* **gone off FÈET#**
> A: so I've gone off FÈET# – .
> d: you've what
> A,B: (– – – laugh)
> B: he's **gone off *FÈET#***
> A: ***I'm*** **no longer Peter's FÒOTMAN#** (– – – laughs) (2.4:1065–74)

Both *gone off FÈET* and *FÒOTMAN* are ambiguous. In this context *FÈET* means 'rhythmical units' in prosody. Therefore 'footman' can either be interpreted literally as 'man servant' or as 'one who studies prosodic feet'. That 'footman' can have these two meanings is immediately obvious to insiders; to the outsider the double meaning may be inferred from the context. What makes this 'new information' easy to process for B is the fact that he already possesses the adequate background assumptions. His processing effort is consequently minimal, and the utterance is relevant.

Factors influencing discourse function

The term 'discourse function' refers to what an item does in the discourse from a pragmatic point of view.

Position and function

Discourse function is related to 1) position in the turn and 2) position in a sequence of turns.

Position in the turn

Single words and word combinations have a different function depending on whether they occur at the very beginning of a turn, as the second item within the turn or at the very end. Compare *OK* and *right* in different positions:

[27] **Beginning the turn**
B: that ə:m − − Bill PÓTTERTON# wants us to go round
on Sunday AFTERNÒON# .
A: OK̀# YÈS# that's FÌNE# (7.2:91–5)

[28] **Second position**
A: I'll see you at HÒME# .
B: YÈS# OK̀# it's about seven THÌRTY# ́ISN'T it#
(7.2:655–58)

[29] **Within the turn**
A: THÁT'S it#   the   FÒLKLORE {SOCÍETY library#}#
YÈS# that's that's RÍGHT# that's ((FÌNE))# . YÉAH#
RÌGHT# . ə:m well N=OW# ... (3.3:217–24)

[30] **Within the turn**
A: ... and now SÙDDENLY# that half is GÒNE# − −
OK̀# |ai| it's FRÉEZING# but it's FRÍGHTENING#
(6.5:310–14)

[31] **End of turn**
B: I want to get the other SÌDE# before half past FÍVE# − .
OK̀# (7.2:232–33)

OK̀ at the beginning of the turn expresses agreement; OK̀ in
second position emphasizes the agreement expressed by YÈS;
OK̀ within the turn introduces a concluding remark; RÍGHT
within the turn finishes a topic; and OK̀ at the end of the turn
asks for confirmation.

In other cases there is an interplay between discourse
strategic and syntactic functions, or a different position involves a
change of function from purely interactive to purely syntactic.
Compare the following pairs:

[32] A: NÒW# . what was I going to DÒ# . seize a
CIGÁRLETTE# − (2.10:513–15)
A: GÒSH# what is he NÒW# (5.9:115–16)

[33] B: WÈLL# . he's just on |ði:| THEÒLOGY depart-
ment# (7.1:1261–63)
A: he's really fitted in ÁWFULLY WÈLL# (1.6:580)

NÒW at the beginning of the turn (in a separate tone unit) is
used as a **transition marker**, introducing a new topic and
changing the direction of the discourse. When placed within the
turn, it is used as a time adjunct, ie a purely syntactic function.

Notice the position in a separate tone unit in the first case. *WÈLL* at the beginning of the turn (in a separate tone unit), serves as a response marker, whereas *WÈLL* in end position serves as a manner adjunct (see further pp 58–63).

Position in a sequence of turns

Turns have a different function depending on whether they come first, second, or third, etc in a sequence of turns. They may, for instance open, continue and terminate a sequence (later to be referred to as 'exchange'; Chapter 2):

		TURNS
[34] B: you're on THÀT#		OPEN
A: NÒ no no# . DÀVE is# .		CONTINUE
B: DÀVE is on that# . ÀH#		TERMINATE
(1.2:1386–90)		

Words and word combinations are also used for different purposes depending on whether they occur in the first or second turn, etc, in a sequence:

[35] **Turn 1**
A: RÌGHT# well let's ə: – – . look at the APPLICÀTIONS#
– . . .
B: M̂# (2.6:440–52)

[36] **Turn 2**
A: well you've got to plunge into LÒNDON#
B: RÌGHT# . there's no point in DÒING that# (1.11:721–22)

RÌGHT in turn 1 (in a separate tone unit) marks the opening of a new phase. *RÌGHT* in turn 2 (in a separate tone unit) initiates a response (see further pp 59–60).

Form and function

Utterance vs discourse act

There is a tendency for the three basic sentence types to correspond to the three basic communicative functions (or discourse acts):

EXAMPLES	SENTENCE FORM	SENTENCE TYPE	COMMUNICATIVE FUNCTION
the door is ÒPEN	S V C	Declarative	Statement
is the door ÓPEN	V S C	Interrogative	Question
ÒPEN the door	V O	Imperative	Command

However, there is no direct relationship between syntactic form and communicative function. Depending on the situation, a declarative sentence (even with a falling tone) can, for instance, very well function as a question:

> [37] A: this is money for the buying of BÒOKS#
> B: YÈS# (3.3:405–06)

The declarative *this is money for* is equivalent to 'is this the money for . . .'. And interrogative sentences often function as (friendly) commands:

> [38] A: will you make sure the water's HÓT# .
> B: YÉS# – – (4.1:621–22)

will you make sure . . . is equivalent to 'make sure please . . .'. If the form of the utterance matches its function, the relationship between the two is said to be **direct**, otherwise it is **indirect**.

Lexical clues

In cases where the syntactic form does not agree with the communicative function the speaker's intention is generally revealed either by lexical or by prosodic clues (especially pitch direction) or both. The use of lexical clues is easy to demonstrate in 'declarative questions':

> [39] A: and then **you'll probably** have enough MÓNEY#
> to do some *travelling ARÓUND#*
> B: *well . YÈS*# (6.2:478–80)

> [40] A: **I don't suppose** you NÈED Old English and
> Anglo-SÁXON#
> B: well NÒ# but . . . (1.5:25–26)

[39] has three question indicators: *probably*, rising and falling-rising tones and the fact that A states something about a 'B-event', ie something that only B is supposed to know. In [40], *I don't suppose* and the rising tone indicate question function.

The most obvious lexical clue is the 'tag' which is appended to a statement to make it a question. And there are numerous other lexical question markers. Similarly, other categories of discourse act have their own lexical markers. *Please*, for instance, is used to mark a request, while *but* marks an objection, and so on. If there are no explicit indicators, the speaker's intention is generally made clear by the context (cf p 26).

Finally, there are the conventional ways of expressing eg offers and invitations and requests by using an interrogative utterance (p 104).

Prosody and function

Tonicity

Tonicity refers to the placement of tone in a tone unit. The same item in the same position but in different turns may or may not carry a nuclear tone. Compare *now* and *NÒW*:

[41a] A: **now** if you could only get THÁT on to tape# that would be very ÌNTERESTING# . (2.5:104–05)

[41b] A: NÒW# . what was I going to DÒ# seize a CIGÁRLETTE# − (2.10:513–15)

Both serve as turn-initiators. But the fact that *now* is unmarked by prosody, whereas *NÒW* is prosodically marked (uttered in a separate tone unit and followed by a pause), turns *NÒW* into a **frame** marking a new stage in the discourse while *now* seems to serve as a mere **starter** (pp 46–7).

Now, compare the next pair:

[42a] A: . . . I think I'm at my peak of thinking right now actually
B: **right** NÒW# (2.9:498–99)

[42b] A: OḰ# . **RÍGHT#** now − ÍF# or INDÌRA# . . . (9.1:629–30)

right NÒW# confirms what A said and it also serves as a time adjunct with *right* used as a modifier of *NÒW* in the adverbial phrase. Notice that the items occur in the same tone unit. *RÍGHT* terminates the aspect of the topic that has been discussed up to that point, while *now* marks the beginning of a new aspect. Notice that the items occur in two separate tone units.

Pitch direction

The direction of the **pitch** (tone) often plays a decisive role. Compare the two examples in the following pair.

[43a] B: ə:m̩ shall we say . would twelve o'clock be
   OKÁY#
   A: LÓVELY#
   B: RÍGHT#
   A: YÈS# (9.1:312–13)

[43b] A: shall we keep those brackets as they ÁRE#
   B: YÈS#
   A: RÌGHT# (9.1:515–17)

RÍGHT (with a rising tone) asks for confirmation, *RÌGHT* (with a falling tone) confirms.

Since the unmarked intonation contour for declarative utterances (with statement function) is falling, while that of interrogatives with inverted word order (and question function) is rising, it follows that a declarative utterance with a rising tone is readily interpreted as a question:

[44] B: there's a CASSÉTTE {GÓES with that#}# .
   A: YÈAH# (3.2:868–69)

Without the rising tone, what B says would have been taken as a statement providing information rather than as a question asking for confirmation.

Context and function

Meanings

As we have already seen, an utterance can have more than one 'meaning'. Here we shall distinguish between the **literal** word-by-word meaning and the **pragmatic** meaning, or function, acquired from the actual context. Literal meaning and pragmatic function may of course agree; ie the speaker may intend exactly what s/he says. If they disagree, on the other hand, it is quite possible to misinterpret what somebody says, going by what was actually said instead of what was apparently meant.

> The **literal** meaning is the sum of the lexical and the syntactic meanings of the utterance in isolation
>
> The **pragmatic** meaning varies with the situational context in which the utterance occurs

The context

Utterances in conversation are not isolated phenomena but depend on the entire context for their interpretation. Exactly what the speaker means by saying something must be interpreted not only in relation to what the previous speaker just said, the **immediate context**, but also in relation to the **wider context**, which includes the speech situation, the topic, the speakers and their relationship to each other, and the knowledge they share about the world.

The speech situation

The speech situation can vary in a number of ways. It can be formal or informal; it can involve talking about everyday matters or highly technical matters; it can involve speakers who are near friends or speakers who have never seen each other; it can be of a private or a public nature, and so on. All this affects the interaction.

The topic

Everyday topics are easy to talk about. No sophisticated vocabulary is needed, and no deep knowledge is required. Topics related to a professional field, on the other hand, not only require adequate knowledge but generally also a certain jargon. Compare, for instance [45] and [46]:

> [45] B: well you see her GRĂNDCHILDREN# don't go to
> see HĚR#
> c: m
> B: so why should it MẮTTER# I mean I might have
> HÛNDREDS of them# and Y=ET#
> D: yeah

B: they probably would never come to SĒE me#
c: because you'll be nice .
D: YÉAH#
c: people go and see nice grandmas
D: YÉS# (1.12:1364–75)

[46] B: ... I mean I think that's *the MĀIN thing*#
A: *((to see))* the state of the ĀRT RĒALLY# they've
just had what they call international hydrological
DECĀDE# . you know in nineteen SIXTY- FĪVE#
{they STĀRTED it#}# with a . special ĒFFORT on
ə:m# RESĒARCH and . all these THĪNGS# . and
this was if you like a progress REPŌRT# at the ĒND
of that period# to S=AY#
C: =M#
A: what if anything they'd ACHĪEVED# – –
C: YĒAH# –
A: you see some of us are |a:| INVŌLVED# . from a
PRĀCTICAL point of view# particularly in . FLŌOD
control# and . IRRIGĀTION {to a lesser EXTÉNT#}#
– so it's interesting to KNŌW# what the state of
the art ĪS# . and where we go from HĒRE# – and
what practical ŪSE it is# ĀNYWAY# (2.8:761–81)

The vocabulary in [45] is extremely general, and technical terms
appear only in [46]. More strikingly, [45] is much more of a
dialogue than [46], where A speaks most of the time. As regards
level of formality, [45] is definitely a 'chat', whereas [46] is more
lecture-like.

Speaker relations
The way we talk depends not only on what we are talking about
but probably even more on who we are talking to. Therefore, the
level of formality does not have to change as a result of the choice
of topic. Even a scientific topic can be discussed in a relaxed way,
here reflected in the use of *you know* and *sort of*:

[47] A: ... they're better REMŌVED# . **YŌU** know# –
there're a very small PERCÉNTAGE# that may
become MALĪGNANT# – become . YŌU know#
neo neoplastic **sort of** GRŌWTHS# . CĀNCERS#
– ə:m S=OME# become INFĒCTED# – and some
YŌU know# get that **sort of** HŌRNY thing# have

you ever seen those HŎRNY things# sticking
ŎUT# . . . (2.9:907–19)

It is no exaggeration to say that we do not talk in the same way
to our closest friend as to a complete stranger, that teenager talk is
different from adult talk, that students do not talk in the same
way to their teachers as to their fellow students, and so on. And
not only is the language different, so is generally the choice of
topics.

Shared knowledge
Shared knowledge is the knowledge that speakers have in
common. Without a certain amount of shared knowledge,
communication would hardly be possible. The type of shared
knowledge required in an everyday chat is, of course, far less
specific than the type required in a conversation about a
specialized subject.

What is and what is not shared knowledge may be crucial
for the interpretation of utterances whose form does not reveal
their function. Compare the following declarative utterances:

[48] A: . . . we did MEDIĔVAL Latin a lot# which I'm rather
GRÀTEFUL for#
B: ÔH# (2.5:495–98)

[49] A: we talked about YŎUR questions#
B: ÒH# (2.5:192–93)

The responses (ÔH, ÒH) reveal that both declaratives are
interpreted as informs, which is only natural. But compare the
next example:

[50] A: in other WÓRDS# you are {NÒT} in a HÙRRY#
—

B: **oh** we're in a hurry to BÛY# because prices are
going to go up . . . (8.2:668–71)

Since we do not normally go around telling people things they
already know, a statement made by A about B or about
something that only B is supposed to know is interpreted as a
request for confirmation (unless it is meant as eg a compliment, a
reproach, or a suggestion or is ironic). Notice that the falling tone
in A's declarative utterance does not prevent it from acting as a
question and that *oh* is now used as a response marker and not as
an information receipt as in [48] and [49].

What A says is ambiguous in isolation, however. In a different context it might be telling B that 'there is no hurry'.

If you want to know more:

General descriptions of conversation include Brown and Yule (1983) Ch.1, Cheepen and Monaghan (1990), Coulthard (1977), Crystal and Davy (1975), Goffman (1979), Nofsinger (1991), Stubbs (1983), Taylor and Cameron (1987) Ch.1, Wardhaugh (1985);

Specific areas are dealt with in other studies eg:

turntaking, in Beattie (1981), Edmondson (1981) Ch.4, Oreström (1983), Roger and Bull (eds) (1988), Sacks, Schegloff and Jefferson (1974);
prosodic units and information structure, in Altenberg (1987), Brown et al (1980), Brown and Yule (1983) Ch.5, Crystal (1969), Quirk et al 1985) Ch.18, Stenström (1990b);
intonation, in Brazil (1985), Brown (1977, 1983);
topical structure, in Bublitz (1988);
conversational structure, in Schenkein (ed.) (1978);
coherence and cohesion, in Brown and Yule (1983) Ch.7, Bublitz (1988) Ch.2, Coulthard (1977), Craig and Tracy (eds) (1983), Halliday and Hasan (1976) Ch.1, Quirk et al (1985) Ch.19, Tannen (ed.) (1984), Thavenius (1983), Tomlin (forthcoming);
signals and markers, in Edmondson (1981), Schiffrin (1987), Stenström (1990a);
adjacency pairs, in Coulthard (1977);
aspects of function, in Brown and Yule (1983) Ch.1, Coulthard (1977), Leech (1983) Ch.7, Quirk et al (1985) Ch.2, Richards and Schmidt (1983), Sinclair and Coulthard (1975);
cooperation, in Brown and Levinson (1978), Grice (1975), Leech (1983) Ch.4, Levinson (1983) Ch.3, Taylor and Cameron (1987) Ch.5;
speech acts, in Austin (1962), Leech (1983) Ch.5, Levinson (1983) Ch.5, Searle (1969);
shared knowledge, in Gibbs (1987), Labov and Fanshel (1977);
relevance, in Sperber and Wilson (1986);
speech situation, in Bailey (1985), Brown and Yule (1983), Leech (1983), Levinson (1983).

CHAPTER 2

Interactional structure

The discourse hierarchy

Spoken interaction can be described in terms of five hierarchical levels, each consisting of one or more units from the level next below:

The TRANSACTION	consists of one or more exchanges dealing with one single topic; one or more transactions make up a conversation
The EXCHANGE	is the smallest interactive unit consisting, minimally, of two turns produced by two different speakers
The TURN	is everything the current speaker says before the next speaker takes over; it consists of one or more moves
The MOVE [ ]	is what the speaker does in a turn in order to start, carry on and finish an exchange, ie the way s/he interacts; it consists of one or more acts
The ACT < >	signals what the speaker intends, what s/he wants to communicate; it is the smallest interactive unit

♣♣♣ Square and angular brackets will be used for [moves] and <acts> throughout the book

The way a brief transaction can be built up is illustrated by the following dialogue, which is part of a lunch-time conversation between a married couple (husband A and wife B). The transaction is made up of two exchanges, one consisting of

two turns (A B) the other of three (A B A). In this example, each
turn consists of one move, while three of the moves contain
more than one act:

[51] TRANSACTION   act   Move

A: [<have you brought my   1   1
    dress SÙIT in#>] – –

B: [<YÈS#> .   1   2   EXCHANGE 1
    <but it's still in the car   2
    at King's CRÒSS#>.]

A: [<well>   1   1
    <can you can you not   2
    get CLÒSER#>]

B: [<yes>   1   2
    <I CÒULD have   2
    DÓNE#>
    <but I didn't THÍNK I   3
    could when I . came   EXCHANGE 2
    ÍN# so I thought well I
    can park it here outside
    the MÈTER ZÓNE#>
    – –
    <it's better than trailing   4
    round looking for a
    MÈTER#>] – – –

A: [<M̌#>] – – –   1   3
    (4.1:78–86)

♣♣♣   '[< . . . >]' indicates a move consisting of one act; '[< . . . >
     < . . . >]' indicates a move consisting of two acts, etc.

The exchanges are part of the same transaction, since they are
both related to what speaker A asked for in the first exchange.
The second exchange would certainly not make sense without
the first.

    Exactly what is done in a transaction can also be illustrated
in the form of a tree diagram, which emphasizes the relation
between the various ranks in the hierarchy:

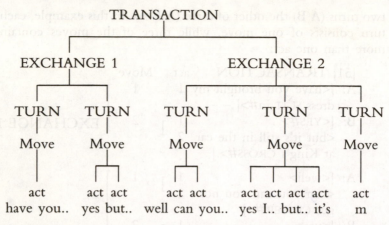

However, some turns consist of more than one move. Consider the following extract from a telephone conversation between two colleagues. In this case the two exchanges, which are part of a somewhat longer transaction, consist of only three turns:

[52] TRANSACTION
A: [<ÒH and# and by the   1   1
    WÀY#>
    <you didn't try using   2   EXCHANGE 1
    your RÉADING-room
    TÍCKET# as a
    STÙDENT card#>]
B: [<NÓ#>] –   1   2

    [<CÓULD I have#>]   1   1
A: [<YÈS#>   1   2   EXCHANGE 2
    <it WÔRKS#> –   2
    <you KNÓW#>]   3
    (7.2:771–78)

The reason is that turn 2 contains two moves; the first move, realized by NÓ, terminates EXCHANGE 1, the second, realized by CÓULD I have, initiates EXCHANGE 2.

A tree diagram of these two exchanges would look as follows:

```
                        TRANSACTION
                             |
              ┌──────────────┴──────────────┐
        EXCHANGE 1                      EXCHANGE 2
             |                               |
      ┌──────┴──────┐                        |
   TURN 1         TURN 2                   TURN 3
      |         ┌────┴────┐                  |
    Move      Move      Move              Move
      |         |         |         ┌────────┼────────┐
   ┌──┴──┐   ┌──┴──┐   ┌──┴──┐   ┌──┴──┐  ┌──┴──┐  ┌──┴──┐
  act   act act   act act   act act   act act   act act
```

by the you didn't NÒ CÒULD I have YÈS it WÔRKS you
WÀY   try using   KNÒW

Both tree diagrams illustrate that transactions generally consist of more than one exchange, each of which involves two or more turns. They also show that exchanges are made up of at least two moves, an initiating and a responding move, each of which consists of one or more acts.

In sum, if the negotiation of a topic is done in one exchange, this exchange constitutes a transaction. If the negotiation stretches over more exchanges, these together constitute the transaction.

The turn, ie what the speaker actually says, is central; what is done in the turn is essential for there to be an exchange in the first place, and for the type of exchange in the second. Therefore, the turn will be the starting-point for further description.

▶▶▶▶ **Now try this!**

The following extracts from admissions interviews in an English department are part of longer transactions. [A] consists of two exchanges. But what about [B]?

[A] a: ə: you can support yourself fully during the course
    A: YÉS#
    a: ə: and you can be a full-time student
    A: and I can be a full-time STÙDENT# YÈS#
       (3.1:27–31)

[B] B: how did you get on with CHÀUCER# .
    A: WÈLL## I LÍKED it#
    B: you LÌKED it# do you REMÉMBER any Chaucer {NÓW}#}# –
    A: ə:m
    B: what did you RÈAD# you read . |ði:| PRÓLOGUE# the TÁLES#
    A: The PRÒLOGUE# {YÈS#}#
    B: well . did you read any of the TÁLES#
    A: YÈS# The PÁRDONER#

B: The PÁRDONER'S# The Nun's Priest's TÁLE#
A: YÈS# (3.1:724–39)

[Answer on p 211]

Five levels

Turns

> The **turn** is everything A says before B takes over and vice versa

A speaker in possession of the turn does not just produce an utterance, s/he also makes at least one interactive move and performs at least one communicative act. The size of turns varies from one word upward, but while it is true to say that the shorter the turn the less is done, the opposite does not have to be true, since a long turn can be just one move consisting of a single act in the same way as a short turn. Consider for instance the following example:

	TURN
[53] B: I think they've got quite a good OPÌNION of him# –	1
A: well ə I I have TÒO#	2
B: Ḿ#	3
A: ə:m – – ((well I mean)) . the way these chaps GÒ#	4
B: MHM# (1.1:592–96)	5

All the utterances in [53], regardless of length, constitute turns in their own right (ie even *M* in this case, cf p 35), and they all consist of moves that carry the dialogue forward.

Simple and complex turns

If only one thing is done in a turn, ie if it contains only one move, it is **simple**; if more things are done and it contains more than one move, it is **complex**. In the extract that follows, two female colleagues are choosing pictures for their respective offices:

[54] A: well LÒOK# . shall I take THÌS#
B: DÒ# (1.4:558–60)

Speaker A does two things in her turn; first she draws B's

attention to a picture she has chosen (*well LÒOK*), then she asks what B thinks about it (*shall I take THÌS*). B does only one thing; she encourages A to take the picture (*DÒ*). In other words, A's turn consists of two moves and is complex, B's consists of one and is simple (cf p 33).

However, a simple turn is not always less intricate than a complex turn. Take the following extract where a young male social worker is telling a colleague about an eleven-year-old girl who went shop-lifting:

> [55] A: I mean I mean she's so LÌTTLE# I mean you you
> KNÓW# sort of one can IMÀGINE# a sort of
> middle-aged WÒMAN# with a coat that seemed .
> you KNÓW sort of# . just slightly exaggerated her
> FÒRM# . you know I mean she could sort of slip
> things in inside PÒCKETS# but ... (2.13:402–09)

The turn is fairly long in terms of words but simple in terms of content and function. A does only one thing, she tells a story. But this does not prevent the turn from being syntactically intricate. Take for instance *I mean you KNÓW sort of one can IMÀGINE* and *a coat that seemed you KNÓW sort of just slightly exaggerated*. The reason for the intricacy is that the speaker has some difficulty in formulating the message and therefore exaggerates the use of verbal **fillers** (*I mean, you KNÓW, sort of*).

Turns and non-turns

Turntaking presupposes a shift of speakers. An utterance produced while the other party goes on speaking can consequently not be regarded as a turn. In [56], A and B produce the same number of utterances, but a different number of turns; there is only one speaker shift, between the first two turns:

		TURN
[56] A:	how how was the WÈDDING#	1
B:	ÒH it was it was really GÒOD# it was ə	2
	it was a lovely DÀY#	
A:	YÈS#	☆
>B:	and . it was a super PLÀCE# . to HÀVE it .	
	of CÓURSE#	
A:	YÈS# –	☆

>B: and we went and sat on sat in an
{ÒRCHARD} at GRÁNTCHESTER# and
had a {HÙGE} TÈA *ÁFTERWARDS#
(laughs – –)* .
A: *(laughs – –)* . (7.3:1444–51)

A's *how how was the WÈDDING* triggers off a lengthy account of what happened. B simply takes over the floor, while A's contributions are restricted to backchannelling. The reason why there are no asterisks indicating simultaneous speech is that both instances of YÈS come at the end of a clause, probably when B draws her breath.

Moves

> The **move** is a verbal action which carries the conversation forward

Move types

The following moves have been identified.

[Summons]	calls the listener's attention
[Focus]	introduces the [initiate]
[Initiate]	opens the exchange
[Repair]	holds up the exchange
[Response]	continues or terminates the exchange
[Re-open]	delays the termination of the exchange
[Follow-up]	terminates the exchange
[Backchannel]	signals the listener's attention

EXAMPLES

[57] [**Summons**]
A: LÒOK now
ə:# you might be going in ÀUGUST# –
B: YÈS# (6.2:579–81)

[58] [**Focus**]
A: **well I'd like to know what you're SÀYING#** about
THÍS#
are you SÀYING# that . the doctor's RECOLLÈCTION#
was completely WRÓNG# . (11.1:332–34)

[59] **[Initiate]**
A: **what did you read ÈNGLISH# or NÒT#**
B: YÈS# I RÈAD ÉNGLISH# (1.5:17–20)

[60] **[Repair]**
A: you're staying HÈRE ÁRE you#
B: ə YÈS# we've got to do a grand TÒUR# .
A: **got to do WHÀT#**
B: a grand TÒUR# (1.5:694–99)

[61] **[Response]**
A: did you read ÈNGLISH# or NÒT#
B: **YÈS# I RÈAD# ÈNGLISH#** (1.5:17–20)

[62] **[Re-open]**
A: ə:m shall we say . would twelve o'clock be ÓK#
B: LÔVELY#
A: RÍGHT#
B: YÈS# (9.1:312–15)

[63] **[Follow-up]**
A: ə: shall I come ÉARLIER# or at four o'CLÒCK#
B: no I should CÒME {at four o'CLÒCK}#
A: **all RÍGHT#** (7.2:167–71)

[64] **[Backchannel]**
A: we had reached the P=OINT# of thinking that we
   weren't going to be able to RÉACH# . a PÓLICY
   decision# *.* and so we
B: ***that's RÍGHT#***
>A: must . tell these GÚYS# that we'll carry ÒN# –
   (1.2:167–72)

Simple and complex moves

As we have seen, many moves consist of more than one act, ie an
obligatory primary act and an optional secondary and/or complementary act (cf p 33). Compare the following examples:

[65] *One-act move*
A: [<locked yourself ÓUT>]# .   [Initiate]
B: [<YÈS>]# (1.2:855–56)   [Response]

The [initiate] and the [response] consist of one primary act each.

[66] *Two-act move*
A: [<did she have glasses as WÈLL>]#   [Initiate]
B: [<YÈS>#   [Response]
<she DÌD>]# – – – (11.1:71–73)

The [initiate] consists of a primary act and the [response] of a primary act (*YÈS*) and a secondary act (*she DÌD*).

[67] *Three-act move*
A: [<have a glass of SHÉRRY>]# .   [Initiate]
B: [<ÔH># ⌢   [Response]
<that's NÍCE of you>#
<as I'm not DRÍVING>]# (1.2:844–47)

The [initiate] consists of a primary act, and the [response] consists of a complementary act (*ÔH*), a primary act (*that's NÍCE of you*) and a secondary act (*as I'm not DRÍVING*).

Moves consisting of more than three different types of act are rare. Exactly what acts do will be dealt with in the next section.

▶▶▶▶▶ **Now try this!**

(a) Identify the moves.
(b) Which are simple and which are complex?

A: I was . I was wondering what we were going to DÒ this weekend# . are you going to do some work on the car TOMÓRROW# – . be an IDÉA# WÒULDN'T it# .
B: I'm not going to do very MÙCH# I'm just going to . hear it RÙN# . (4.1:53–58)

[Answer on p 211]

Acts

┌───┐
The **act** signals what the speaker wishes to communicate
└───┘

There are three different categories of act:

Primary acts	can realize moves on their own
Secondary acts	accompany and sometimes replace primary acts

Complementary acts accompany but rarely replace primary acts

[68] A: have a glass of SHÉRRY# [Initiate<offer>]
    B: ÔH# [Response <uptake>
       that's NÍCE of you# <accept>
       as I'm not DRÍVING# <justify>]
       (1.2:844–47)

A's initiating move consists of one act, a primary <offer>. B's responding move consists of three acts, a complementary <uptake>, a primary <accept> and a secondary <justify>.

Let's imagine that B had responded only by ÔH or *as I'm not DRÍVING*. Only the latter would be a perfectly acceptable primary act (preferably but not necessarily preceded by ÔH), since it can be interpreted as 'yes please' in more or less the same way as *that's NÍCE of you*.

Primary acts

The following primary acts have been identified:

Primary acts	
<accept>	agrees to a <request>, <suggest>, etc
<acknowledge>	signals receipt of information
<agree>	signals agreement with what was just said
<alert>	calls the addressee's attention
<answer>	responds to a <question>/<request>
<apology>	expresses regret
<call-off>	prompts a conversational closing
<check>	asks for clarification
<closer>	ends a conversational closing
<confirm>	responds to a request for confirmation
<disagree>	expresses disagreement
<evaluate>	judges the value of what the previous speaker said
<greeting>	greets somebody or bids farewell
<inform>	provides information
<invite>	asks if somebody 'would like to do X'
<object>	signals a different opinion
<offer>	presents something for acceptance/rejection
<opine>	gives one's personal opinion
<query>	expresses doubt or strong surprise
<question>	asks for information, confirmation, clarification
<react>	expresses attitude and strong feelings
<reject>	disagrees to a <request>, <suggest>, etc

<reply>	responds to a <statement>
<request>	asks somebody to do something
<smoother>	responds to an <apology>
<statement>	informs or expresses opinion
<suggest>	puts forward an idea or a plan
<thanks>	expresses gratitude

♣♣♣ <question> is an umbrella term for <identification question>, <polarity question> and <confirmation question>

<request> is an umbrella term for <action request> and <permission request>

<answer> is an umbrella term for <comply>, <imply>, <supply>, <evade> and <disclaim>

EXAMPLES:

[69] <accept>
A: MÁISIE will you have another one#
B: **oh YÈS#** THÀNK you# ((how)) LÒVELY# (4.3:925–28)

[70] <acknowledge>
A: . . . our MÁTHS chap# our junior MÀTHS chap up THÉRE# he's an ÎNDIAN# .
B: **MͪM#** (1.6:493–96)

[71] <agree>
A: they seem to know their way ARÓUND#
B: **so it DÒES seem#** . . . (1.5:785–86)

[72] <alert>
A: LÒOK now# (6.2:579)

[73] <answer>
A: you got a CÓLD#
B: **– NÒ# . just a bit SNÍFFY#** (1.3:6–8)

[74] <apology>
A: Ì said no more than ((usual))
B: ÀH# . **I'm SÒRRY#** (7.2:854–56)

[75] <call-off>
B: no I should CÒME {at four O'CLÒCK#}#
A: all RÍGHT#
B: **ÀLL right#**
A: SÈE you# (7.2:169–73)

[76] <check>
A: were you there when they erected the new SÌGNS# –
B: WHÌCH new signs# (5.9:50–51)

[77] <closer>
B: ... OḰ# thank you very MÙCH#
A: RÍGHT#
B: RÌGHT# GOODBỲE# (8.1:616–20)

[78] <confirm>
A: and Hart you've got to stand ÙP to# HÀVEN'T you# .
B: YÈS# I've gathered THÀT# ALRÉADY# . (laughs)
   (1.5:117–22)

[79] <disagree>
A: I I can see that COMPLÈTELY# – ə:m
B: but not for HÌM you can't#
A: oh YÉS# . I M=EAN# . ...(6.5:1036–40)

[80] <evaluate>
A: ... you throwing a PÀRTY#
B: YÈS#
A: that's GÒOD# (1.4:12–15)

[81] <greeting>
A: *hello*
B: *HELLÓ#* . sorry I'm late# (2.7:1–3)

[82] <inform>
A: you're next on my PHÓNE list#
B: oh RÉALLY# (7.3:1314–15)

[83] <invite>
A: would you like to take some LÙNCH . *young
   PÁULINE#*
B: *M̀# ....* (6.2:1038–39)

[84] <object>
A: ... there's no RÈASON why it should *be so
   surprising#
B: *well but they were SURPRÌSED# (2.8:589–90)

[85] <offer>
A: anybody have some more CÒFFEE#
B: no I don't I WÒN'T have anymore# (4.3:1147–48)

[86] <opine>

A: **and I mean it's the most ÓBVIOUS press# – ÉVEN more obvious than CÀMBRIDGE#**

B: yes but your bibliography is not such an obvious scheme as as ə:m . as the ə:m – as the reprint series (2.1:254–56)

[87] <query>

A: ə:m – but does that MÈAN# that you're not going on a ə:m {VÍSITOR'S} VÍSA# .

B: yes I ÀM#

A: **you ÀRE going on *a* visitor's VÍSA#**

B: *YÈS#* well you see I'm trying to get a FÙLBRIGHT# . (6.2:289:294–95)

[88] <question>

A: **did you meet any ǓNDERGRADUATES# in your * – * STÀY#**

B: *oh NÒ*# (1.3:1074–76)

[89] <react>

B: did you *RÉALLY#*

A: *MHM#* –

B: **good LÒRD#** (6.2:908–10)

[90] <reject>

A: anybody have some more CÒFFEE#

B: **no I don't I WǑN'T have any more#** (4.3:1147–48)

[91] <reply>

A: you're next on my PHǑNE list#

B: **oh RÉALLY#** (7.3:1314–15)

[92] <request>

A: **would you be good enough to let me KNÓW# when Mr Buckram will be available on the TÉLEPHONE#** (9.3:1257–58)

[93] <smoother>

A: thanks for PHÒNING#

B: sorry it wasn't last NÌGHT#

A: **oh that's all RÍGHT#** (7.2:1096–98)

[94] <statement>

A: (laughs .) . **you're next on my PHǑNE list#**

B: oh RÉALLY# (7.3:1314–15)

[95] <suggest>
A: it doesn't mean ÀNYTHING# . to NÌNETY per cent of
   the people who come out HÚNTING#
B: **then why not have a DRÀG hunt#** . (5.6:666–68)

[96] <thanks>
A: **many THÀNKS#**
B: RÌGHT# (9.1:165–66)

▶▶▶▶▶ **Now try this!**

This extract, which consists of two exchanges, contains six
different types of primary act. Try to identify them:

A: I don't think you've BÈEN upstairs YÉT#
B: only just to the LÒO#
A: YÈAH# – ə: well . Sidney HÈATH {sort of *lives*
   UPSTÀIRS#}# but he's really
B: *Y=ES#* =M#
A: seems to work more with . HÁRT#
B: YÈAH# (1.5:730–39)

[Answer on p 211]

Function and form

As was pointed out in Chapter 1, the speaker does not always
mean what s/he literally says, and the listener cannot always
identify the speaker's intention by the form of the utterance.
Function is not simply a matter of surface structure but a matter
of WHEN and WHERE something is uttered, by WHOM and
for WHAT PURPOSE. The fact that the following interrogative, for instance, does not function as a <question>, as the form
suggests, but as a <request> is clearly reflected in the [response]:

[97] A: can you tell mum ((I'll)) be LÀTE# – .
     B: **all RÌGHT#** (7.3:133–34)

A direct <answer> to a *yes/no* <question> would have been
realized by *yes* or *no* (or a variant) and not by *all right*.

  Misinterpretations are rare, however, since the speaker's
intention generally follows from the actual speech situation.
Interestingly, utterances interpretable in more than one way can
be extremely convenient, especially as a means of getting out of
an awkward situation. Speakers do not seem to exploit their
opportunities to use such 'unfair' strategies, however.

Secondary acts

The following secondary acts have been identified:

Secondary acts	
<clue>	follows a primary act and gives a hint
<emphasizer>	underlines what was said in the primary act
<expand >	gives complementary information
<justify>	defends what was said in the primary act
<metacomment>	comments on current talk
<precursor>	precedes a primary act and gives information
<preface>	introduces a primary act

EXAMPLES

[98] **<clue>**
A: – – – where did you hear THÁT# . **you must have
coined this YOURSÈLF#** (1.1:529–30)

[99] **<emphasizer>**
A: ə: as you KNÒW# . the CÀR'S been {STÒLEN#}# .
B: oh yes **of CÒURSE#** (5.9:244–46)

[100] **<expand>**
A: ə so you know this area quite WÈLL#
B: YÈS# **it was just . off MÒNTAGUE Street some-
where#** . (5.9:763–65)

[101] **<justify>**
A: is THÁT good for you# .
B: a Wednesday is QUÌTE a good day# **cos I don't teach
at ÀLL on it#** (9.1:670–72)

[102] **<metacomment>**
A: W=ELL# MÂY I ask# **what goes ÌNTO that paper
NÔW#** (1.1:8–10)

[103] **<precursor>**
A: **I would like to use it again TONÌGHT though#** . do
you think you could ask either HÍM# or VÈRA#
(7.2:72–74)

[104] **<preface>**
A: **but what made you DECÌDE#** – did you go from
UNIVÈRSITY to SECRETÀRIAL *school# ə*

B: *YÈS#*
A: AUTOMÀTICALLY# (5.9:294–97)

It is very often the position of the act in the move that distinguishes a secondary act from a primary act. Consider, for instance, the function of *that's right* in the two versions of [105]:

[105a] (fabricated)
A: so I should direct the second year students exactly the same way as the FÍRST ones#
B: YÉS# . **that's R ÌGHT#**   [<confirm><**emphasizer**>]

[105b] (genuine)
A: so I should direct the second year students exactly the same way as the FÍRST ones#
B: **that's RÌGHT .** # YÈS# –   [<**confirm**><emphasizer>]
(9.2:379–81)

The change of places leads to a change of functions; YÈS, which originally served as a primary act <confirm> turns into a secondary act <emphasizer> and the secondary act *that's RÌGHT* is converted into a <confirm>.

Compare also the two versions of [106] and you will notice that the same string of words is used both as a secondary act <expand> and a primary act <confirm>:

[106a] (genuine)
A: ə so you know this area quite WÈLL#
B: YÈS#   [Response<confirm>
    it was just . off MÒNTAGUE Street   <expand>]
    somewhere# (5.9:763–65)

[106b] (fabricated)
A: where ÌS this area#
B: **it was just . off MÒNTAGUE Street** [Response<**confirm**>]
    somewhere#

In the genuine version, the <confirm> is realized by YÈS. In the fabricated version, YÈS has been left out, and *it was just . off MÒNTAGUE Street somewhere*, which served as an <expand> in [106a] has now taken over the role as primary act. It confirms the <suggest> indirectly since it presupposes that B knows the area.

▶▶▶▶▶ **Now try this!**

Identify the secondary acts in the following extract:

[a] A: you're staying in HÈRE ÁRE you#
    B: YÈS# we've got to do a grand TÒUR# (1.5:694–
       95)

[b] A: I looked at some of my *PÓRTRAITS* and .
    B: *M̌*
   >A: grotesque as they may BȆ# they . capture some
       ÁSPECTS of *REÁLITY#*
    B: *{WÈLL}* I'm SÙRE# . YÈS# – – – (1.8:273–78)

[Answer on p 212]

Complementary acts

The following complementary acts have been identified:

Complementary acts	
<appealer>	invites feedback
<booster>	assesses what the speaker himself says
<empathizer>	'involves' the listener
<filler>	fills a gap in the discourse
<frame>	marks a boundary in the discourse
<hedge>	helps avoiding commitment
<monitor>	helps putting something right
<staller>	plays for time
<starter>	helps getting started
<uptake>	accepts what was said and leads on

EXAMPLES

[107] **<appealer>**
A: it's not really in LÌNE# with your PRÒMISE **you
   KNÓW#** –
B: NÒ# (4.1:626–28)

[108] **<booster>**
A: and DÒN'T# **for heaven's** S=AKE# . believe all you
   read in the PRÈSS# (5.4:1373–75)

[109] **<empathizer>**

A: he was NÈW here THÉN# . new BÀCK here# **you KNÓW#** (1.6:700–02)

[110] **<filler>**

A: ə:m =AND ə:# – we WÈLL# **I mean you KNÓW# I mean** I do TRÝ and do something about THÍS# (3.3:970–73)

[111] **<frame>**

B: and we ÒFTEN# . very FRÉQUENTLY# – talk about maximizing the PRÒFIT# – – **N=OW#** – certainly in ÈASTERN Europe# – – one has a different IMPRÈSSION# (6.1:801–06)

[112] **<hedge>**

A: I didn't MÈAN to I didn't MÈAN to sound . **sort of** (. laughs) PRÍSSY# (6.2:37)

[113] **<monitor>**

A: ə:m I had sort of mixed FÈELINGS ABÓUT it# Ì didn't ə WÈLL **I mean** I I suppose cos I was a bit STÙPID# . (7.1:892–93)

[114] **<staller>**

A: ə:m – – – WÈLL# – – – the THÌNG about this . {NÒVEL#}# . . . (3.1:284–85)

[115] **<starter>**

A: how relèvant is your – programme to THÍS kind of THÍNG#

B: **well** we . DÒ have# . əm in the . ə MÀCRO MÁRKETING# . ə part of the CÓURSE# (6.1:542–45)

[116] **<uptake>**

A: because she told me that she'd been taught never to NÒTICE# what she ÀTE# .

B: **oh** . WÈLL# . I was always . always pə ə: HÚNGRY# (6.4:853–56)

Complementary acts are typically realized by a fairly limited set of lexical items (*you know, I mean, right, sort of, well, oh* etc), many of which can also serve as primary and secondary acts (for a complete list of items see p 208). The exact interpretation depends not only on where they occur but also on how they are pronounced (their intonation contour). One important place is at the end of a turn, the position of the <appealer>. Compare, for instance, the two different functions of *right* in the same turn-final position:

[117a] (genuine)
A: I'll let I'll be in TÓUCH#
B: YÈAH# . DÒ that# . OKÁY# . RÌGHT# (7.3:913–17)

[117b] (fabricated)
A: I'll let I'll be in TÓUCH#
B: YÈAH# . DÒ that# . OKÁY# . RÍGHT#

The falling tone on *right* in [117a] indicates that nothing more has to be said on the subject (<frame>). The rising tone in [117b] indicates that B expects A to confirm the agreement (<appealer>). Another important strategic place is the beginning of the turn, the position of the <uptake>:

[118] A: they did an UNDERGRÁDUATE ə . they were UNDERGRÁDUATES together#
      B: **oh** I know that Mick Grew did his MÀ in London# but I didn't know he was an UNDER-GRÁDUATE here# − (5.9:999–1001)

Here, it is both the lexical realization of the item (**oh**) and its relation to the immediate context that decide its function.

▶▶▶▶▶ **Now try this!** (the example is slightly modified)

Complementary acts occur in three places. Can you spot them?

A: I mean I don't know any English or LINGUÌSTICS# so I was just . you just accept things to TÝPE# because you know EVÈNTUALLY# you have to sort of . sort things out YOURSÈLF#

[Answer on p 212]

Exchanges

The **exchange** is the minimal interactive unit and involves the negotiation of a single piece of information

Simple and complex exchanges

In the simplest case the exchange consists of two turns, each containing one move, [initiate] and [response], respectively. This is the normal pattern for stating exchanges. Questioning exchanges, by contrast, and also requesting exchanges, often contain a third turn consisting of an evaluating [follow-up] move.

Stating exchange

A: he ìs Muslim#   [Initiate]
B: M̀# (1.6:565–66)   [Respond]

Questioning exchange

A: and D'YÓU . teach –   [Initiate]
B: NÒ# Ì DÓN'T# because I'm not ÈNGLISH at all#   [Respond]
A: Ì see# – – (1.5:457–61)   [Follow-up]

Requesting exchange

A: can you hold ÒN a minute   [Initiate]
B: M̀# (8.2:1145–46)   [Respond]

♣♣♣ Requesting replaces commanding since <commands> occur extremely seldom in conversation

All three types of exchange may be more intricate, both as regards the length and complexity of turns and the combination of moves into exchanges. By and large, the longest turns are found in stating exchanges, while the more complex turns and move combinations are found in questioning and requesting exchanges.

One reason for the relative complexity of questioning and requesting exchanges is that they are often preceded by an introductory 'pre-exchange', where the speaker makes sure that necessary pre-conditions hold before getting to the point:

---

[119] B: but ə you're teaching . əm at a GRÀMMAR school#
ÀREN't you#
A: YÈS# *YÈS#*

> B: *well* what do you think about SÈX education# .
>   (5.10:382–86)

A second reason for complexity is that the answerer may need a clarification of the <question> before s/he can answer:

[120] A: ə ((one)) wouldn't ə: have the NÊRVE# to take
         THÁT one# WÓULD one#

> | B: | **what that NÙDE#.** |
> | A: | YÈAH# |

B: YÈS# well it's sort of TÒO . YÈS# (1.4:473)

B could not possibly have answered before she knew which of the pictures A was referring to.

A third reason for complexity is that the <answer> is often followed by the questioner's evaluation or confirmation, which may be further commented on by the responder:

[121] B: how long does it go ÒN for#
      A: ə:m it goes on for seven twenty-five to eight
         FIFTÉEN#

> | B: | **that's not TÒO frightful#** |
> | A: | NÒ# |

(9.1:802–05)

A fourth reason for complexity is that the speaker can end one exchange and begin a new exchange in the same turn:

[122] A: ə:m so that the first WÈEK I had *((everyone .*
         coming in on MÈ))#

> | D: | ***ə:m . FRÌGHTFUL# .** |
> | | **why did you LÈAVE# .** |

A: ə:m . MÁINLY# cos I'd been there two . two
   YÈARS#
D: M̀# . (1.5:1245–52)

Finally, the complexity of an exchange may also be the effect of the speaker's roundabout way of structuring the message:

[123] A: **well NÓW#**
         if this is a FÀCT# .

TH=EN# is it a BÓRE# . to go to some other part
of the LÍBRARY# which isn't necessarily ÈNGLISH#
– cos there's nobody in the LÌBRARY# to say
you're ÈNGLISH# you've got to sit THÈRE#
B: not RÉALLY# NÒ# (3.3:169–79)

Here A proceeds stepwise. He starts by framing off the new
exchange from what preceded (*well NÓW*), showing that he is
ready for a conclusion. The conclusion (*if this is a FÁCT*), serves to
focus on what is to come, namely a <question>. And, the
introduction can be even more complex, as we shall see in
Chapter 3.

Exchange patterns

Stating and questioning exchanges form various patterns.

Stating exchanges

The following patterns are typical of stating exchanges:

Chaining		Supporting	
A:	⌈ S1	A:	⌈ S1
B:	⌊ R1	B:	☆
A:	⌈ S2:	>A:	S1
B:	⌊ R2:	B:	☆
		>A:	⌊ S1

♣♣♣ S = <statement>
    R = <reply>
    ☆ = <acknowledge>

In a **chaining** sequence, A initiates the first exchange and goes
on to initiate the next exchange:

[124] A: ⌈ S1 not only is there a green light showing up a
           man – WÁLKING# . but there's pip pip pip
           pip pip pip pip pip PÍP#

      B: │ R1 that's TRÚE# I've come across THÓSE# I
           └   didn't know what they were FÒR# –

      A: ⌈ S2 well that's ÍT# they're for people with
           poor SÍGHT#

      B: ⌊ R2 YÉAH# – – – (2.14:516–24)

The speakers' contributions are fairly equal in length, speaker changes are frequent, and neither of the speakers has a clearly dominating role. In other cases, one speaker dominates for some time while the other plays a subordinate role, and after some time the roles are reversed.

The clearest case of speaker domination is found in story-telling where the story-teller does all the talking supported by [backchannels] from the other party/parties. Here, A tells a couple of friends about the way she acquired a sewing-machine, by writing a manual:

[125]   A: . . . and I was quite HŎNEST about it# I said
            you know I . I haven't used one for YÈARS#
            and they said . you're just the person we
            WÀNT# because ((the)) person who . HÀSN'T .
            {ÙSED one#}# ((and))
       B: *=M#*
   >A: has to have it all DĚMONSTRATED# *.* will
            understand the PRÒBLEMS#
       B: *m*
   >A: *.* better than an ÈXPERT# *–* so I DÌD the
            thing# . . .
       B: *m* *m* (1.3:111–22)

Questioning exchanges
These are the most typical questioning-exchange patterns:

chaining		embedding	
A: [q1		A:	q1
B: a1		B: [q2	
A: [q2		A: a2	
B: a2		B: a1	

coupling		elliptical coupling	
A: [q1		A: [q1	
B: a1+q2]		B: (a1) q2	
A: a2		A: a2	

♣♣♣   q = <question>; q1 = first <question>, etc.; a = <answer>; a1 = <answer> to first <question>, etc.

In a **chaining** sequence A initiates the first exchange and goes on to initiate the next one:

[126] a: ⌜ q1 are you normally free Tuesdays#
B: ⌞ a1 I'm normally free TUÈSDAY#
a: ⌜ q2 and Thursdays#
B: ⌞ a2 and THÙRSDAY# (7.1:1109–12)

In an **embedding** A's initiating move is followed by a querying subordinate exchange before B terminates the superordinate exchange:

[127] A: q1 that wasn't the guy I MÈT# WÀS it# –
when we SÀW the BÚILDING# –
B: ⌜ q2 saw it WHÈRE# –
A: ⌞ a2 when I went over to Chet*wynd RÒAD#*
B: a1 *YÈS# –* (4.2:193–99)

The embedding is an example of **discontinuity**, ie a temporary hold-up which is often necessary for the completion of an exchange.

In a **coupling** sequence A's initiating move is followed by a turn in which B both responds to what A just said and initiates a new exchange:

[128] A: ⌜ q1   ÒH and# by the WÀY# you didn't try
using your RÈADING-room TÍCKET# .
as a STÙDENT card# – – .
B: ⌞ a1+q2 NÓ# – CÓULD I have#

A: a2   YÈS# (7.2:771–77)

In an **elliptical coupling** B's [response] to what A said can be implicitly derived from the way B goes on to the new exchange:

[129] A: ⌜ q1   well d'you know what they GÓT#
B: ⌞ (a1) q2 WHÀT# –

A: a2   they didn't get REPLÍES from . from
most PÉOPLE# – (4.1:790–92)

There is no explicit <answer> to *d'you know what they GÓT*. But there is no doubt that B means 'no' without saying it.

Requesting exchanges

Most <requests> are expressed in the interrogative form. Some are expressed by a declarative or an imperative. The exchange patterns are more or less the same as for questioning and stating exchanges. The following patterns are characteristic:

chaining		embedding	
A: ⎡ q1	pre-	A: ⎡ <request>	
B: ⎣ a1	sequence	B: ⎡ q1	
A: ⎡ <request>		A: ⎣ a1	
B: ⎣ <accept/reject>		B: <accept/reject>	

The **chaining** sequence is typically introduced by a **pre-sequence** preparing the way for the <request> (the example is abbreviated):

[130] A: ⎡ q1 ə have you been to have a LÓOK# .
       B: ⎣ a1 no I haven't been to look NÓW# . . .
       A: ⎡ <request> would you be G=OOD enough# . to
       | have a look . . .
       B: ⎣ <accept> YÈS# . . . (3.3:371–79)

Another typical pattern is the following example of embedding, where B does not comply with the <request> until a potential misunderstanding has been cleared away:

[131] A: ⎡ <request> can I speak to JÍM Johnstone
       | PLÉASE#
       B: | ⎡ q1 SĚNIOR#
       A: | ⎣ a1 YÈS#
       B: ⎣ <accept> YÈS# – – –
                         (9.1:1133–36)

A declarative <request> might give rise to the same exchange pattern but also the following, elliptical coupling:

[132] A: <request>   I'd like to be put on your
                         MÀILING-list *PLÉASE#*
       B: <reject>   *we* don't RÚN a mailing-list#
       A: <acknowledge> ÓH# (8.2:15–17)

Stating, questioning and requesting strategies will be dealt with in Chapter 3.

▶▶▶▶▶ **Now try this!**

What exchange pattern(s) does the following sequence represent?

A: ə:m do you and your husband have a CÁR#
B: – have a CÁR#
A: YÈAH#
B: NÒ# –
A: ÒH# . how do you move ABÒUT#
B: by tube or a BÙS or whatever# . you KNÓW#
A: how very PLEBÈIAN# – – (8.2:335–43)

[Answer on p 212]

Transactions

> A **transaction** consists minimally of one exchange dealing with one topic, but usually of a sequence of exchanges dealing with the same topic

Simple transactions

Simple transactions, consisting of a single exchange, are most likely to occur in brief face-to-face encounters and especially brief telephone calls where the caller leaves a short message, asks for information, or makes a simple <request>:

[133] A: Professor Clark asked if you were . going to collect some SCRÍPTS {TONÍGHT#}# *|i| SÒUND* scripts# .
B: *YÈS#* ((MHM))#
A: if you'd collect them from Mr GÒRDON# *who will be going to* |ði:| PLÀ meeting#
B: *Mr GÓRDON#* – YÈS#
A: RÍGHT#
B: Y=ES# (9.1:718–25)

Here we have an indirect <request> (*if you were going to collect . . .*
if you'd collect) which is accepted (*Mr GÓRDON# YÈS*)#
whereupon the agreement is confirmed (*RÍGHT# Y=ĚS#*).

Complex transactions

Some transactions are long. Some are both intricate and long.
The following transaction, which consists of five exchanges, has
only eight turns. One might have expected at least ten turns,
since an exchange consists minimally of an initiating and a
responding move. But remember that a turn is not always
equivalent to a move, but can consist of more than one move,
which is exactly what happens in some of the exchanges in this
transaction, where B goes on in the same turn after reacting to
what was said:

[134] TRANSACTION	Turn	Move	Exchange
B: **is there any MÍLK#** – .	1	1	
A: ((yeah there's)) this this ə POWDER((ED)) milk#	2	2	1
B: ⌃AH yes# –	3	3	
what does that do in TÈA# does that DISSÓLVE in tea#		4	2
A: I've only just DISCÓVERED that# ə a week AGÒ#	4	5	
B: **((we)) used to have that in the WÀR#**	5	6	3
A: I had it in CÒFFEE# . *ÈARLIER#*	6	7	
B: *M#*			
>A: **the thing =IS#** that it's quite H=ANDY# if you run ÒUT of *milk#*		8	4
B: *QUÌTE#* YÈAH#	7	9	
will it *MÈLT* ((in tea though))# .		10	5
A: *((it KÈEPS))#* I SUPPÒSE SÓ# – – it's dehydrated MÌLK# . (1.4:126–45)	8	11	

All the exchanges except 2 and 3 are linked together by overlapping turns, ie the same speaker terminates one exchange and initiates another in the same turn. Pay special attention to turn 6 where ('>' shows that) A is still holding his turn after the backchannelling M̌ inserted by B.

Summing up, simple transactions, consisting of a single exchange, are likely to occur in telephone enquiries, service encounters (eg when buying something in a shop), and casual interchanges (eg when meeting somebody very briefly in the street). Complex transactions, consisting of two exchanges or more, are far more common in conversation in general.

▶▶▶▶▶ Now try this!

Analyse this brief transaction in terms of moves and acts:

    A: ə:m do you and your husband have a CÁR#
    B: – have a CÀR#
    A: YÈAH#
    B: NÒ# –
    A: ÒH# . how do you move ABÒUT#
    B: by tube or a BÙS or whatever# . you KNÓW#
    A: how very PLEBÈIAN# – – (8.2:335–43)

                            [Answer on p 212]

Summing up five levels

When speakers take turns they make interactive moves which build up exchanges. The maximal configuration of the exchange is the following, with two subordinate exchanges (repairing and re-opening):

    [135] (fabricated)
    A: look John   [Summons]
       there's going to be an interesting   [Focus]
       discussion at the meeting this afternoon
       will you be there   [Initiate]

B:	what time	[Repair]
A:	5 o'clock	[Response]

    B: OK   [Response]

| A: | are you sure | [Re-open] |
| B: | yes | [Response] |

A: good   [Follow-up]

Exactly what is intended by what is said is expressed in the **acts** that the moves consist of.

If the negotiation of a topic is done in one exchange, this exchange constitutes a **transaction**. If it stretches over more exchanges, these together constitute one transaction.

▶▶▶▶▶ **Now try this!**

This questioning sequence contains four moves and six acts.
[a] Identify and label the moves and acts.
[b] Decide what type of exchange pattern is represented.

A: has Ivor gone HÓME# –
B: I THÍNK so#
A: has the sixth form conference FÍNISHED then#
B: YĚS well# . it finished really last NÍGHT# (4.1:1013–17)
[Answer on p 213]

Interactional signals and discourse markers

An inventory

Some lexical items are so frequent and are used for so many purposes in conversation that they merit a section of their own. I am thinking of items like *yes*, *sure* and *gosh*, which are purely interactive; *you know*, *please*, and Q-tags, which appeal directly to the listener; *well*, *I mean* and *sort of*, which help the speaker to start and keep going; and *anyway* and *now*, which help the speaker to organize her/his speech.

All the items listed below serve as acts in moves, but due to their specific properties, it might be helpful to view them in terms of **interactional signals** and **discourse markers** to begin with (for definitions, see pp 61, 63).

The most common lexical items		
actually	I think	right
ah	mhm	sort of
all right	no	sure
anyway	now	Q tag
God	oh	that's right
goodness	OK	yes/yeah
gosh	please	you know
I mean	quite	you see
I see	really	well

It is important to keep in mind that the same lexical item can do more than one thing, depending on where it occurs in the discourse, and that it can sometimes do two things at once. Therefore, in order to interpret what an item does one has to take note of its position.

Function and position

What a particular lexical item does is strongly related not only to where it occurs in a turn but also to whether it makes up a turn of its own and whether this turn comes first, second, third (or later) in the exchange:

> [136] A: shall we keep those brackets as they ÁRE# –
> B: YÈS#   [Response<answer>]
> A: RÍGHT# (9.1:515–17)[Follow-up<acknowledge>]

An item that makes up a turn of its own is also a move consisting of one act. Consequently YÈS is not only an <answer> but it constitutes the whole [response] move, and RÍGHT is not just an <acknowledge> act but makes up the entire [follow-up] move.

In longer turns with a move (moves) containing a string of words, the lexical item concerned is no more than an act in a move:

> [137] A: ... and I will ... – go into your financial
> RAMIFICÁTIONS# ÁLL RIGHT#   <appealer>
> B: RÌGHT#   [Response<agree>]
>
> OÍK# I'll have it . I'll have it down   <frame>

> in DÈTAIL# exactly what we earn and HÒPE to earn#
> ÁLL RIGHT#   <appealer>
> A: ÓH# .   <uptake>
> **well** l I don't worry about THÁT#   <starter>
> (8.2:906–17)

The beginning and end of a turn are strategic points. This is where speakers 'link up with' each other, so it is not surprising to find specific interactional signals in those positions. Notice how ÁLRIGHT links up first with R ÌGHT and then with ÓH.

Other strategic points are found within the turn; what items do there is important for the organization of the discourse. This is the place for 'stage markers', or <frames>:

[138] A: TH ÀT'S it# the FÒLKLORE {SOCÌETY library#}#
YÈS# that's RÍGHT# that's ((FÌNE))# . YÈAH# –
RÍGHT# . ə:m . **well N=OW#** |j| you you SÀY in
ÓTHER words# . . . (3.3:217–25)

R ÌGHT marks the end of a discussion (about the difficulty of getting a seat in the library) and *well NÒW* marks the beginning of a summing up of what has been said.

A fairly reliable way to the understanding of what interactional signals and discourse markers do is to view them as filling a gap in the exchange, ie as a turn of their own, and as slot fillers in the turn:

Gap fillers
EXCHANGE

A: _____	Turn 1
B: _____	Turn 2
A: _____	Turn 3
(etc)	

Slot fillers
TURN

Slot 1	Slot 2		Slot 3	Slot 4		Slot 5
		wwwwww			wwwwwww	

♣♣♣ 'wwwww' = lexical content other than lexical items used as interactional signals and discourse markers

The following characteristics of signals and markers should be kept in mind:

* they can fill more than one gap in the exchange
* they can fill more than one slot in the turn
* they can do different things in different places
* they can do different things in the same place

Interactional signals

> **Interactional signals** are used to start, carry on and terminate the conversation

Interactional signals appeal for feedback (eg RÍGHT) and give feedback (eg I SÈE), they respond (eg YÈS that's RÌGHT), they involve the listener in the conversation (eg YÒU know), and so on. In other words, they play a crucial role for a smooth interaction.

Interactional signals as gap fillers

The majority of the items listed in the inventory can occur in a turn of their own, except in turn 1 for obvious reasons. *Right*, which can occur in all three places, is a good example.

[139] Turn 2
A: . . . it's ÚNDER – H for HÀRRY#
B: **RÌGHT#** (8.2:109–11)   [Respond]

[140] Turn 3
A: ə:m shall we say . would twelve o'clock be OḰ#
B: LÒVELY#
A: **RÍGHT#**   [Re-open]
B: YÈS# (9.1:312–15)

[141] Turn 4
A: so what time are you CÒMING this afternoon#
B: əm . |əwə| as we said about four O'CLÒCK#
A: OḰ# YÈAH# .
B: **RÌGHT#** (7.2:114–18)   [Follow-up]

Notice how the function changes depending on whether the item occurs in the the second, third, or fourth turn of the exchange. Somewhat unexpectedly, *RÌGHT* as a [follow-up] appears in turn 4. This is because *OK# YÈAH* in turn 3 is the [follow-up] of the [response], *as we said about four O'CLÒCK.* Consequently, *RÌGHT* in turn 4 becomes a second [follow-up]. Usually, there is only one [follow-up] in an exchange, ie in turn 3.

Interactional signals as slot fillers

Lexical items serving as interactional signals are found in slots 1, 2, and 5, ie turn beginnings and ends, but generally not in slots 3 and 4, which are typically filled by items serving as discourse markers. Function varies with position. Consider *right* again, which happens to be one of the most versatile items:

[142] Slot 1
A: RÍGHT#
B: **RÌGHT#** and keep an eye out for something<confirm> for for . ÈMMELINE# (7.2:145–47)

[143] Slot 2
A: I'll see how I GÒ#
B: OÃ# **RÌGHT#** (8.3:528–29)   <emphasizer>

[144] Slot 5
A: you were going to get ÒUT of MÁRRIAGE# . and DÌDN'T – – – **RÌGHT#** – – (6.5:851–53) <question>

Remember, however, that *right* has other functions; it can also be used, for instance, as an <appealer>, an <accept> and an <answer>. And, as we shall see in the next section, it can serve as a discourse marker.

▶▶▶▶▶ **Now try this!**

The following extract contains as many as nine interactional signals (including *GRÈAT*). What exactly are the signals used for?

A: . . . is this Chris's CÁR#
B: NÓ# I don't know WHÒSE car it'll *be*
A: *UHÙH#*
B: I don't THÌNK it'll be Chris's#
A: M̀#

B: but . I'll be {THÈRE} directing TRÁFFIC#
A: OK# . RÌGHT#
B: OK#
A: GRÉAT# – YÉAH# . WÈLL# – see you THÈN# . *that's
    WÓNDERFUL*
B   *all RÍGHT# see you FRÌDAY#*
A: RÌGHT# (7.2:1395–1412)

[Answer on p 213]

Discourse markers

> **Discourse markers** are used to organize and hold the turn and to
> mark boundaries in the discourse

Discourse markers help the speaker organize the discourse. They
serve to start a conversation; they serve to introduce and mark the
end of a topic; they serve to introduce a digression and mark the
resumption of the old topic; and they signal the end of a
conversation.

Discourse markers as slot fillers

Discourse markers are typically found in turn slot 1 and turn slots
3 and 4 and occasionally 5. They serve as <frames> and
sometimes <starters>:

[145] Slot 1
A: **RÌGHT#** well let's ə: – – . let's look at the
    APPLICÀTIONS# (2.6:440–41)

[146] Slots 3 and 4
A: well I WÈNT about quarter TÓ# *(– laughs)*
B: *very* SÈNSIBLE# – **RÌGHT#** well I I probably WÒN'T
    see you# but ə: (7.3:75–80)

In slot 1, the <frame> RÌGHT marks the beginning of a new stage
in the discourse. The <frame> RÌGHT in slot 3 ends the
discussion, while the <starter> well in slot 4 introduces a
concluding comment.
    Other items with similar functions are anyway and now.

[147] Slot 1
A: (– – laughs) ÀNYWAY# see you TONÍGHT# (7.1:858–59)

[148] Slot 4
A: they will only have to SÉND them# – to one PLÀCE# – – NÒW# . if their costs are going to be REDÚCED # ... (6.1:1036–39)

[149] Slot 5
A: well that was exactly what she DÎD say# (laughs – –) . and (laughs – –) ÀNYWAY# əm (4.1:108–10)

Notice that, when *now* and *well* are used as <frames>, they occur in a separate tone unit.

We have seen that *right*, *anyway* and *now* can all be used as <frames>. But due to their inherent meanings they are not doing exactly the same thing. This becomes evident if we try to replace one by the other. Generalizing somewhat, *right* looks backward, *now* looks forward, while *anyway* looks both ways.

Irregulars

A mixed lot of lexical items fall out of the slot-filler framework when they serve as:

* <empathizers>
* <hedges>
* <stallers>
* <fillers>

You know and *you see* are used as <empathizers> to engage the listener and make her/him feel part of the conversation. They often appear at the beginning and end of a turn, but, as [150] illustrates, also elsewhere, for instance when the speaker appeals for feedback:

[150] A: he's not a RELÀXED lecturer# but he's . a DRÌVING lecturer# **you KNÒW#** – whereas SÒME of them here# stand ÙP poor DÉARS# and they haven't the first CLÙE# – they're so NÈRVOUS# **you KNÒW#** {PÀINFUL} to LÌSTEN to# (1.6: 752–60)

If *you know* had been left out, the facts would have been the same, but the effect of A's utterance would not have been the same. What A said would have sounded more matter of fact and probably less friendly, and the listener might have felt less involved.

Items like *actually, I think, really,* and *sort of* are used as <hedges>, the effect of which is to modify and mitigate an utterance:

[151] A: and I've got . several FLŎWER people#
       B: ooh ə |ðae| that's nice .
       A: oh it ÌSN'T ÁCTUALLY# (7.1:205–07)

Lexical items of this type tend to cooccur, and collocations like the following are common:

[152] A: whereas HÁRT# **I mean as you KNÒW# sort of** –
          – (1.5:622–24)

The long pause that follows indicates that the speaker is at a loss. Consequently, items that are used as <hedges> can also be used as <stallers>.

In some cases, it is not at all obvious what the items are doing. Are they simply used as <fillers>, for want of something better to say?

[153] A: he he he just TÀLKS# NON-STǑP# RĚALLY# .
          ((ÁCTUALLY))#}# (7.2:543–45)

Strategies where these devices are used will be dealt with in more detail in Chapter 3.

▶▶▶▶ **Now try this!**

The following signals and markers have been deleted from the extract below: *kind of, in a WǍY, I mean, WASN'T it, I think, you see, sort of.* Try to reinsert them in their original places:

       A: I find it rather DĬFFICULT# to assess # . Eileen has
          moved into a very – rather ǑUTBACK PLÁCE# – and as
          a RESÙLT# she doesn't – – – expect perhaps – – the
          – – SUCCĚSSES {I SUPPǑSE that#}# – – when we lived
          in the PǑTTERIES# in our YǑUTH# – even to
          know ÀNYBODY who wrote a BǑOK# was quite
          SǑMETHING# . (1.13:12–20)

(Remember that the dashes (–) and dots (.) indicate pauses.)

[Answer on p 213]

Summing up signals and markers

The lexical items listed above were typically used for the following functions in relation to their position in the exchange and in the turn:

Moves in EXCHANGE

[backchannel]
[re-opener]
[follow-up]
[<call-off>]

Acts in TURN

Slot 1	Slot 2		Slot 3	Slot 4		Slot 5
___	___	wwwwww ___	Slot 3	Slot 4	wwwww ___	Slot 5
<uptake>	<emphasizer>		<frame>	<frame>		<appealer>
<answer>						
<reply>						
<closer>						

And this is how the various functions were typically realized:

Own turn	[backchannel]	I see, mhm, really, right, yes
	[re-opener]	really
	[follow-up]	right
	[<call-off>]	OK
Slot 1	<uptake>	oh, well, yes
	<answer>	no, right, sure, yes
	<reply>	I see, mhm, oh, right
	<closer>	right
Slot 2	<emphasizer>	that's right
Slots 3 & 4	<frame>	all right, anyway, now, OK, right
Slot 5	<appealer>	all right, OK, Q-tag, right

We have seen that *well*, *I think*, tend to appear at the beginning and others, eg *you know*, *you see*, at the end of the turn. Other items have a less fixed position. What they all have in common is that they make the conversation more smooth, more lively, and more intimate. But if overused, they have a negative effect.

Obviously, it is not possible to classify the lexical items into clearcut functional categories. This seems to be as close as we can get:

[154]

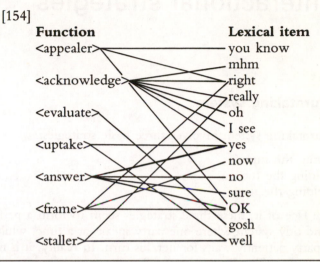

Function	Lexical item
<appealer>	you know
	mhm
<acknowledge>	right
	really
<evaluate>	oh
	I see
<uptake>	yes
	now
<answer>	no
	sure
<frame>	OK
	gosh
<staller>	well

If you want to know more:

Models of analysis are provided in Sinclair and Coulthard (1975) for classroom interaction, and Edmondson (1981) for simulated two-party dialogue. The model suggested by Sinclair and Coulthard (1975) is further elaborated on in Coulthard and Montgomery (eds) (1981);

ways of analysing ordinary, spontaneous interaction are described in Coulthard (1977), Levinson (1983) Ch.6, Roger and Bull (eds) (1988), Stubbs (1983), Taylor and Cameron (1987) Ch.3;

ways of analysing question–response sequences are described in Merritt (1976), Stenström (1984);

models of analysis for language teaching are outlined in McCarthy (1991);

interactional signals and discourse markers are described in Aijmer (1984, 1986, 1987), Erman (1987), Schiffrin (1987), Schourup (1985), Stenström (1990a), Östman (1981).

CHAPTER 3
Interactional strategies

The turntaking system

The turntaking system involves three basic strategies:

* taking the turn
* holding the turn
* yielding the turn

On the face of it, these three strategies seem to form a perfectly neat and tidy system where one party speaks at a time, while the other party patiently waits for her/his turn. In reality, it is not as simple as that. The listener may fail to be as openly attentive as s/he is expected to be, with the result that the conversation peters out for lack of encouragement, s/he may butt in without waiting for the current speaker to finish, which results in overlapping turns and interruptions, or the speaker may lose the thread, which causes an unwanted silence if the listener is not prepared to fill the gap.

By and large, however, speaker and listener do pay attention to each other, and smooth speaker-shifts are far more common than unsmooth ones (p 35).

Taking the turn

Taking the turn can be tricky. The speaker may not have done the necessary planning and is not ready to go ahead, as reflected in [155]:

[155] B: əm . well . ə . he used to be my tutor# . . .
(5.9:80)

Turn beginnings can also be revealing from another point of view; the very first word may announce whether the speaker

agrees to, doubts or objects to what the previous speaker said.
Compare, for instance, the following beginnings:

[156] a **yes** I DÌD know once a FRÈNCHMAN# ...
      b **well really** I I'm just SÀYING# that ...
      c **but** OFFÍCIALLY# he never changed ...

Moreover, a distinction can be made between turns that are
topically related to the previous speaker's turn and those that are
apparently not and between turns that are explicitly linked to the
previous speaker's turn and those that are not.

Taking the turn may involve:

* starting up
* taking over
* interrupting

Starting up

A speaker who has not done the proper planning before taking
the turn will either have to play for time or give up the turn at
once. In the opposite case there is no great problem. The speaker
can just go ahead. In other words, starting up can involve:

* a hesitant start
* a clean start

A hesitant start

Most speakers do not give up the turn at once but take advantage
of available stalling devices.

Filled pauses (əm, ə:m) and **verbal <fillers>** (eg *well, I
mean, you know*) come in handy when the speaker takes the turn
without being fully prepared. They show that s/he intends to say
something but needs more time to put it into words. Therefore,
they tend to cluster in the 'global planning area' at the very
beginning of a turn, where the rough planning of the entire
utterance takes place:

[157] B: WÈLL# ə:m . I **mean** that is . the most
         obvious |ə̀n| ə: EXÁMPLE# but ə: ə − . if they
         talk about UNEMPLÒYMENT# .
      d: m
      B: they'll S=AY# − − the UNEMPL=OYED# they
         should be made to do . some . some WÒRK# and
         not . scrounge off the STÁTE# (2.11:556–63)

Notice the two successive hesitation strings, the first (*well ə:m . I mean*) followed by B's comment on what the previous speaker said, the second (*but ə: ə – .*) preceding the rest of the utterance.

The extract demonstrates very clearly that silent and filled pauses and verbal <fillers> occur in combination and that they can consequently do the same job in the conversation (for other uses of *well, you know, I mean, etc* see pp 58–67).

Combinations of pauses and <fillers>

ə:m –
ə:m well/well ə:m
ə:m – – but . you know
ə:m – well I mean . you know
well I mean –
well ə:m you know/you see
well now – let me see

Two other lexical items that are often met with in the planning area at the beginning of the turn are *actually* and *obviously*:

[158] A: ((**actually**)) I'm going to to |ði:| ə:m . ði: ə:m ði əm ði əm ði əm TURNER thing {with GERALD#}#
       (7.2:732)

Why *actually*, one may wonder, other than as a way of getting started?

[159] A: I said to ə:m . Steve . and COMPANY# to come –
       . you KNOW# . sort of after SEVEN# . we
       B: MHM#
       A: ə OBVIOUSLY# we we probably aim to –
       EAT# at – . you KNOW# soon after EIGHT#
       (7.2:970–78)

If something is probable, can it then also be obvious? OBVIOUSLY is obviously doing the same job as *actually* in [158], ie it serves as a turntaker.

A clean start
Surprisingly often, speakers use an introductory device <**starter**> to begin the turn, although no more planning is involved, and some speakers do so more often than others. The typical <starter> is realized by *well*:

[160] A: **well** what does he SÀY# – stick an initial label on
the BÀCK# (1.4:566–67)

It is as if some kind of takeoff is needed. Or *well* is used as a
linking device:

[161] A: **W=ELL#** . MÁY I ask# what goes ÌNTO that
paper NÓW# (1.1:8–10)

Other strategies used to introduce [initiates] in exchange openings
will be dealt with in Chapter 3.

Taking over

Subsequent turns may be explicitly connected by an <uptake> or
a link.

<Uptakes>

By an <uptake>, which occurs in [response] and [follow-up]
moves, the next speaker acknowledges receipt of what the
previous speaker said and evaluates it before going on. The
<uptake> is often triggered off by an <appealer> in the previous
speaker's turn, as in [162], where A has just got a telegram from a
person who suffers from varicose veins:

[162] A: but I got a telegram last ə:m .   [initiate]
FRÌDAY# – .
SÀYING# that there was trouble AFÒOT#
you KNÓW#
B: **YÈAH#** – . trouble a LĔG ÀNYWAY# [response]
(8.4:660–65)

The <appealer> is realized by *you KNÓW*, the <uptake> by
YÈAH. By contrast, the next extract, from a discussion about
conditions in prison, has no <appealer>:

[163] A: . . . if you're in there and you're   [initiate]
ŎN remand# you're TĚASED# for
not being . an actual . CÒNVICT#
B: and you're not ə TÒUGH ((e*nough))#*
A: *ŎH#* you're not YŎU know# [response]
you're not a MÀN# (4.7:209–14)

[164] illustrates that both a [follow-up] and the preceding
[response] can be introduced by an <uptake>:

[164] A: but why was Chetwynd Road so   [initiate]
CHÉAP# – – –

B: **ah** that . there is an answer to THÁT#   [response]
–

nobody could get a MÒRTGAGE on
it#-

A: **oh** THÀT'S right {YÈAH#}# – –[follow-up]
(4.2:304–07)

<Uptakes> introducing <answers> are usually realized by *oh*
and *well*. But *oh* and *well* are not doing exactly the same thing.
Compare [165] and [166]:

[165] A: but |ə| HÒW did you {FÌND it#}# at at ə .
SECRET=ARIAL school#

B: **oh** it was ÀWFUL# . it RÈALLY was# .
(5.9:253–56)

[166] A: are you in TÒUCH with the St {BÉE'S} CRÓWD#
or

B: **WÈLL#** you KNÒW# . to a certain EXTÉNT#
(1.9:81–85)

One difference is that *oh* tends to initiate <answers> to *wh*-
<questions> and *well* <answers> to *yes/no*-<questions>. Another
difference is that *oh* signals emphasis, while *well* signals hesitation,
reservation and indirectness.

<Uptakes>
ah
no
oh
well
yes

♣♣♣ <Uptakes> are very often not in a nuclear position

Links
Links are realized by lexical items that are labelled conjunctions
(*and*, *but*, *cos*) and conjuncts (*so*) in the grammar and which
connect sentences and clauses. Obviously, they have an important
interactive function as well:

[167] A: don't MISUNDERSTÀND me# I'm very FÒND of
Diana Dors#

> B: **but** she's not two hundred years O̬LD#
> A: no by golly and neither am I̬# (5:1:622–25)

Links, like <uptakes>, introduce a primary act together with which they form the initiating move in the turn. Links can, for instance, introduce an <object>, as in the previous example, or an <inform>:

> [168] A: you ME̬T her#
>   B: . NO̬# – NO̬#
>   A: **cos** she I̬S UNU̬SUAL# – – – (1.3:1200–03)

or a <question>:

> [169] B: we interviewed . up to about SI̬X# .
>   a: yes m – –
>   B: the last ((one was SI̬X))#
>   A: **so** you've NE̬VER |ə| I M=EAN ə:# you haven't
>   been in the HA̬BIT of# ə: interviewing MA̬NY .
>   candidates# (2.6:461–66)

Links
and
but
cos
so

♣♣♣ Links are usually not in a nuclear position

Interrupting

The most obvious reasons for interrupting are the following: B has got the impression that A has nothing more to say; B thinks that s/he has 'got the message' and that there is no need for A to elaborate; or B wants to speak up at a particular point in the ongoing talk, before it is too late. Any of these reasons can result in competition for the turn:

> [170] A: . . . well his manner APPE̬ALED to me# .
>   B: M̬#
>   A: YE̬S# ⋆((I . I))⋆
>   B: ⋆I can see that⋆ if you DI̬DN'T#
>   ⋆ə . get O̬N with it#⋆

    A: *yes QÙITE# SÒME PÉOPLE#*
        əm Beryl MÀRTIN {for ÌNSTANCE#}# (1.5:126
        –34)

By *I can see that*, which overlaps with *I I* in A's preceding turn, B
manages to silence A and take over the turn. But A takes revenge
almost immediately by *yes QÙITE# SÒME PÉOPLE#*, which
overlaps with ə . *get ÒN with it#* in B's turn. The result may
seem confusing to the outsider, but the speakers involved have no
difficulty in understanding each other, judging by the rest of the
conversation.

  Some discourse devices are excellent interruptors, notably:

* <alerts>
* <metacomments>

Alerts
<Alerts> are intended to attract the other party's/parties'
attention. Therefore, they tend to be louder than the surrounding
context and are generally uttered with a higher pitch:

  [171] A: oh well that's very good if you can fool him just
          for an instant – – *((2 to 3 sylls))*
        B: *LÌSTEN# ((if* you)) feel like a FÌLM tomorrow
          night MÌKE# – (1.7:1206–08)

LÌSTEN forces A to stop speaking although he has obviously
more to say.

  However, <alerts> do not always have the intended effect:

  [172] A: now at LÈAST *I've got something* now I've got
        B: *HÈY# I've got*
      >A: something to S=AY# (4.2:1–4)

A has already begun announcing that he has got something to say
and does not pay the slightest attention to B's effort to get a word in.

+--------------------+
| **<Alerts>** |
| |
| hey |
| listen |
| look |
+--------------------+

♣♣♣ <Alerts> are pronounced in a separate tone unit and with a
    falling tone

<Metacomments>
The situation may demand that we do not just butt in:

[173]   A: əm – but more important than THĂT# . *since it's
        really a matter of NOMĔNCLATURE#*
        B: *could I halt you there* could I halt
        you there and answer that point FÌRST# –
        (5.3:139–41)

In this extract from a radio discussion, it would not only have
been extremely impolite of A not to let B in but also entirely out
of place.

    <Metacomments>, so called because they actually comment
on the talk itself, are polite devices, which allow the listener to
come up with objections without appearing too straightforward
and without offending the current speaker. In other words, they
have a **face-saving** effect. Clearly, <metacomments> are
particularly common in formal situations, such as business
meetings and serious discussions.

<Metacomments>

can I just tell . . .
can I say something about this
could I halt you there
may I halt you
let me just . . .

♣♣♣   <Metacomments> occupy a separate tone unit; the tone is
typically rising if the form is interrogative and falling if the form
is imperative

Holding the turn

To hold the turn means to carry on talking. But since the
planning that the speaker did at the beginning of the turn may
not be sufficient for the whole turn, and since it is difficult to
plan what to say and speak at the same time, s/he may have to
stop talking and start replanning half-way through the turn.
Silence should of course be avoided, unless it is strategically

placed; the listener might mistake it for a take-over signal. In other words, the speaker has to play for time.

Stalling

The following devices help the speaker avoid a breakdown and take-over:

* filled pauses and/or verbal <fillers>
* strategically placed silent pauses
* repetition
* a new start

Filled pauses and verbal <fillers>

Filled pauses can usually be taken to indicate that the speaker has no intention to yield the turn but is actually planning what to say next:

> [174] A: ... everyone was . PRÒMISED their LÉAVE#
> {ÀND} GÒT it# on the DÀY# and there was
> no MÒNKEYING {ABÒUT#}#
> – ə:m – . so WÈ were RECÙRRING#...
> (1.14:853–56)

Without the filled pause ə:m B could easily have got the impression that A had completed the message, that he had nothing more to say and was ready to give up his turn.

As we saw earlier in this chapter, filled (and silent) pauses tend to cooccur with verbal <fillers> in the hesitation area at the beginning of the turn. Pauses and verbal <fillers> also combine in planning areas within the turn:

> [175] A: ... and ÀLL this was DÓNE ə:# – – by – – kind
> of letting – ə: – – . {WÈLL} RÉALLY by just ə:
> – – sort of ə# – starting from NÒTHING# (2.3:
> 115–17)

The pauses (both filled and unfilled) are accompanied by *kind of* and *sort of*, which usually serve as <hedges> (p 46), by the <filler> WÈLL, which typically serves as a [response] marker, and the adverbial RÉALLY. What *really* does from a purely syntactic point of view is questionable, but from a discourse-strategic point of view it serves as a <staller>. Other items that are used in a similar way are *actually* and *obviously* (pp 207–8). The fact that *actually*, *obviously* and *really* occur together with 'ordinary' hesitation items

makes it appropriate to refer to them as <stallers> just as much as
well, *I mean* and *you know* in that environment.

> [176] A: ə:m – ə: ə there was no damage done at A͡LL#
>   – they had |ð ði:| the CHÁP# had **obviously** –
>   əm *ə*
>   B: *SÒRRY#* just a MÌNUTE David# (5.11:744–
>   48)

What A is referring to is obviously not at all obvious to B, who
simply interrupts.

Silent pauses

A silent pause placed in a syntactically and semantically strategic
place, ie a place where it is evident that the turn is not complete
and that there is more to come, acts as a turn-holder. The
following is an extract from a critical discussion about the
organization of the British nation:

> [177] B: those PÓSTS# . are always FRÈE# . or filled by
>   DÙNDERHEADS# –. during ə PÉACETIME# –
>   a: then we . lose *the first few battles*
>   B: *when –* then you . lose the first
>   few BÀTTLES# . then you SÀCK these fools#
>   like *Lord*
> >B: GÒRT# and people like THÀT# during the last
>   WÀR# . and ÌRONSIDE# and people like
>   THÌS# you KNÓW# the old PLÒDDERS#
>   A: M̀#
>   B: **and** SÙDDENLY# – – – the more brilliant people
>   APPÈAR# . (2.3:726–38)

A very long pause, like the one after *SÙDDENLY* (– – –), would
most certainly have caused a shift of speakers if it had occurred in
a different position, but silence immediately after a conjunction
and an adverbial not only makes it clear that there is more
information to come; it also strongly emphasizes that information.

Lexical repetition

Lexical repetition can involve single words:

> [178] A: . . . . ((cos)) I mean it doesn't make any
>   DÌFFERENCE# **if if if if if if** you've got five

thousand QUÌD# . ə five thousand quid is no
GÒOD to you# if everything. CÒSTS # . fifty
per cent more than it DÌD# . (2.2:688–92)

or clause partials:

[179] A: . . . and he said well how old do you think this
CHÍLD is you SÉE# – – – and I didn't have a
CLÙE# . you SÉE# **it was a it was a . it was it
was** an ÁSIAN child# between the age of . it was
STÁNDING up# so therefore it was thirteen
MÒNTHS# . to FÓUR YÈARS# (2.9:213–19)

or combinations:

[180] A: . . . an awful lot of it ÌS# a lot more English .
than ÈNGLAND# – – – |ai| **I mean they YÒU
know# they they they they they** say {VÈST
meaning} ÚNDERGARMENT# (1.10: 311–14)

In [178] speaker A makes it very clear that he wants to go on
speaking, by repeating the conjunction *if* not once but four times;
and in [179] A finally manages to complete the sentence
beginning by *it was*. The silent pause in [180] is very long, and it
may seem surprising that neither of the two listeners takes over
the turn. The reason is probably that they are both eager to hear
more about Australia, where neither of them has been. There is
no doubt that the speaker is trying to gain time, as reflected in *I
mean* and *YOU know* and the repetition of *they*.

New start

To avoid getting completely lost the best solution may be to
make a new start:

[181] A: but I feel SÒMEHOW# . the sheer FÀCT# of not
having to have . to have . this . really sort of – –
it's **for one thing it does NÁRK me#** that . . .
(4.3:8–11)

Obviously, A had not made up his mind exactly what to say
when he started objecting. He has a hard time trying to put his
thoughts into words by means of repetition, pauses and verbal
<fillers> before he finally realizes that the only way out of the
troublesome situation is to start all over again.

Yielding the turn

As we have seen, eg in examples [170] and [172], there are cases where the speaker has to give away the turn rather reluctantly, but usually, s/he yields the turn without much protesting. The speaker might even appeal to the listener for a [response].

Prompting

Some discourse acts prompt the other party to respond more strongly than others. That turns them automatically into turn-yielders. Such acts are, for instance, <greetings>, <questions> and <requests>:

> [182] C: ((WÉLL# . have we DECÌDED THÉN))# . the grand
> TÒUR#
> B: *YÈS#*
> A: *you're staying* HÈRE ÁRE you#
> C: ə: YÈS# we've got to do a grand TÒUR#
> (1.5:690–96)

The fact that C pays no attention to B's YÈS, which answers his own <question>, and answers A's interruptive <question> instead is one of many examples of <questions> being effective turn-takers. The reason for C's negligent behaviour vis à vis B is that he is compelled to respond, since a <question> always requires an <answer> (cf adjacency pairs, pp 17–18).

Prompting acts
<apology>
<greeting>
<invite>
<object>
<offer>
<question>
<request>

Appealing

A turn-final <appealer> serves as an explicit signal to the listener that some kind of feedback would be appropriate. The 'prompting force' of <appealers> varies from fairly weak, eg when realized by *you know*, to fairly strong, eg when realized by ÓK:

[183] A: and Blundell is a rather cosy old FĬLM MÁN# **you**
KNÓW#
B: YÈS# (9.1:1105–07)

The <appealer> is strongest when uttered after a silent pause,
where it has a questioning effect:

[184] A: I want to get the other SĬDE# before half past
FĬVE# – . ÓK# .
B: YEÀH# (7.2:232–35)

┌─────────────────────────┐
│ **<Appealers>**   │
│   │
│ Q tags   │
│ all right   │
│ right   │
│ OK   │
│ you know   │
│ you see   │
└─────────────────────────┘

♣♣♣ <Appealers> occur in a separate tone unit with a rising tone

Giving up

Giving up involves either that the speaker realizes that s/he has
no more to say or that s/he thinks it is time the listener said
something. In the unproblematic cases, turns are yielded at a
completion point, ie a point where prosody converges with
syntactic and semantic completion and which should therefore
serve as an efficient hint for the listener to take over. If s/he does
not take the hint for some reason, there will be a pause, and the
longer the pause, the stronger the pressure on the listener to say
something:

[185] A: ((and they)) sort of hand it over to the POLĬCE#
who DISPÒSE of it in# the way they think FĬT#
– – –
B: it's like ÊLLA# and Henry's FLĬCK-KNIFE#
(2.13:360–64)

Finally, B takes the hint and goes on.
In other cases it is obvious that the speaker would have liked
to continue:

[186] A: if I if I work quite WÈLL# I can do about
{THRÈE} . a DÁY# – – ə:m – .
B: I didn't RÈALIZE# you were working so closely
with the CÒRPUS# – . (4.6:149–53)

Speaker A makes a final effort, signalled by ə:m but has to give
up, and B takes over.

Summing up the turntaking system

The three main strategies in the turntaking system, taking,
holding and yielding the turn, would undoubtedly be much less
manageable without certain 'help resources'.

Pauses and <fillers> help the speaker to play for time;
<appealers> and <uptakes> help to achieve smooth turntaking;
links help to connect speaker turns; [backchannels], finally, help
the current speaker along while manifesting the listener's
attention.

Backchannelling

Spoken interaction requires active participation by both parties in
a two-party dialogue. This means that the current listener is not
allowed to remain passive. Nor is s/he allowed to provide only
silent feedback, such as head-nods, smiles, and eye-glances. Some
kind of oral responding is expected, minimally in the form of
[backchannels].

The feedback gradient

[Backchannels] can reflect empathy, enthusiasm and indignation,
but they can also reflect a lack of interest, indifference and
impatience, although such feelings are generally expressed in a
different form. Exactly what [backchannels] do is partly a function
of the lexical items chosen, partly of the intonation contour
adopted. Compare for instance [187] and [188]:

[187] A: every WEEKÈND# the children {sort of EXPÈCT}
CHÒCOLATE cake# –
B: =M#
A: and this was a BÌND# . specially when I was
WÒRKING# up till late *FRÌDAY anyway# and
they

C: *=M#
B: YÈAH#*
>A: wanted* a fresh CHǑCOLATE cake# − ə:m − but
   NǑW# you know# there's a CǑUPLE of chocolate
   cakes *in the*
B: *M̌ `#*
>A: FRÈEZER# . (4.3:173−86)

Neither B nor C seems over-enthusiastic. Notice especially the
two instances of =M, reflecting something very close to
indifference.

   In [188] B does not seem to be much affected by A's story
to begin with, judging by the two instances of the minimal
[response] M̌

   [188] A: . . . and I'd got the ((PRǏCKLES)) all night#
        B: M̌#
        A: I couldn't keep STǏLL# and I − I didn't want him
           to TĚLL them# and I didn't had no ǍPPETITE#
           for FǑOD#
        B: M̌#
        A: ((I)) staggered THRǑUGH it# − flew back home the
           next DÀY# . whisked into this HǑSPITAL#
        B: GǑODNESS#
        A: but ə |ðə| that's all RǏGHT# they can {CÙRE}
           MALǍRIA# (1.9:1214−26)

It is not until A mentions HǑSPITAL that B is roused to show
sympathy (GǑODNESS).

   [Backchannels] can be seen along a gradient, ranging from
indifference to strong involvement:

←——————————————————————————————→

indifference   **involvement**
=M   I SÈE   ǑH   GǑSH   RĚALLY   my   GǑODNESS   HÈLL

[189] illustrates two less common variants. Notice the tones:

   [189] A: . . . it's a PǏTY ǍCTUALLY# that the other
           speaker is WÀSTED# because there's *a LÒT . *
           of the
        B: *I KNǑW#*
        C: other speaker ÁCTUALLY#
        B: M̂ADDENING#.
        C: who presumably was ÉRIC# (2.5:1107−12)

Laughter, finally, is perhaps the most frequent type of [backchannel], generally speaking. This episode from a women's college speaks for itself:

[190] >A: ... and I found myself LOÒKING# into this –
             grey moustached FÁCE# *– (– – laughs)*
       b,c: *(– – – laugh)*
       >A: absolutely shapeless WÓMAN# with – you
             KNÓW# no LÌPS on the edge of her mouth#
       b,c: (– – – laugh)
       >A: and she was S=AYING# . the TRÒUBLE# with
             these PÈOPLE# – who advocate mixed CÒL-
             LEGES# . is that they have ABSOLÙTELY#
             NÒ# – – UNDERSTÁNDING# for the {NÈEDS}
             of MÈN# (1.3:719–34)

[Backchannels]	
ah	good heavens
oh	I see
mhm	of course
yes	oh dear
sure	oh God
quite	that's nice
right	that's not bad
really	that's right

▶▶▶▶▶ **Now try this!**

How are turntaking, turnholding and turnyielding strategies represented in the following example? Remember that some contributions are not considered turns.

		line
A:	ə it's absolutely BÀRMY# you can hold the top – –	1
	administrative job in CÒLLEGE# and if you haven't got	2
	a DEGRÉE# – .	3
B:	*((RÈALLY))#*	4
>A:	*you just* can't set foot beyond a certain . you	5
	KNÓW#	6
B:	but if you've got a DEGRÉE# this is MÀGIC# .	7
C:	M̀# . YÈS#	8

A: this is ((a)) battle that I'm always FÍGHTING# that ə a   9
     DEGRÉE# does NÒT# QUÀLIFY you# –   10
B: {ÒH} NÒ# ((I))   11
>A: particularly for *ÀNYTHING#*   12
B: *well one's AWÁRE* of that# YÈS#   13

                                        (1.5:966–83)
                                   [Answer on p 214]

Exchange procedures

In this section we shall proceed stepwise through all the possible
moves in the exchange, from the opening [summons] to the
terminating [follow-up].

Opening

Exchange openings differ in complexity depending on how well
the speakers know each other, what they are talking about, and
the aim of the conversation. And there is a fourth aspect, namely
whether the conversation is private or public. [191] is an extract
from a lunch chat between husband A and wife B; [192] is from a
radio interview with a former Prime Minister:

[191] **Husband-wife**
A: **what are you doing this AFTERNÒON#**   [Initiate]
B: I'm going HÒME# I've got to TÈACH# – – (4.1:5–6)

In this private and informal dialogue dealing with fairly trivial
everyday matters there is no need for polite or explanatory
introductory moves. A goes straight to the point.

[192] **Reporter–Prime Minister**
A: Prime MÍNISTER# .   [Summons]
   the tone of the speech Mr CÀLLAGHAN   [Focus]
   made . {this WÈEK#}# . struck many
   PÉOPLE# as . notably more ACCÒMMODA-
   TING than his FÍRST# – RENEGOTIÁTION
   speech# on April the FÍRST# –
   does that reflect a . shift of INTÉNTION#   [Initiate]
   . on your government's PÀRT# (6.3:
   878–85)

Here, the situation is different. This dialogue is public. It deals with public matters and is intended for a large audience. Therefore, it is not only much more formal than the previous dialogue but also more complex in terms of introductory procedures. It starts by an opening [summons] (*Prime MÌNISTER*) and is followed by a rather long [focus], before the initiating <question> is asked.

Altogether three types of introductory procedures can precede the [initiate]:

* summonsing
* framing
* focusing

Summonsing

One effective way of calling a person's attention to changes in the discourse is by using an <alert>:

> [193] A: RÎGHT# {Î} WÎLL#
> B: (– laughs)
> A: **LÒOK#** . you CÒMING {ÌN#}# SÒON#
> (7.3:45–50)

LÒOK makes A aware that the conversation will take a new direction. At the same time it strengthens the force of the subsequent <question>, and it becomes very difficult for B to avoid answering.

Vocatives, realized by a proper name or some other form of address, fall into this category, as we saw in [192].

Framing

Another way of calling the listener's attention, although perhaps not as effective as summonsing, is framing. <Frames> are often used to signal that a message is on the way or that there will be a change of topics. *Well* and *now*, often in combination, are typically used for this function:

> [194] A: **WÈLL now#** switching to . ə: your return to this
> CÒUNTRY# ... (3.2:102–03)

> [195] A: **well NÒW#** . as . Dennis Danby and Í# .
> maybe SÀID I THÍNK# ... (5.6:13–15)

<Frames>

all right
anyway
now
OK
right
well

♣♣♣ <Frames> are usually pronounced in a separate tone unit with a falling tone

Focusing

A third, somewhat different way of calling the listener's attention is focusing on what is to come by using one of the following devices:

* <metacomment>
* <preface>

<Metacomments>

Since <metacomments> have already been dealt with (pp 44, 75), I shall only give one example at this point. Notice the softening effect:

> [196] A: **I hardly like to SĂY this#** in view of your
> **rude REMÁRKS#** but əm . could you give me
> another RECOMMENDĂTION# (6.2:307–09)

<Prefaces>

Like <metacomments>, <prefaces> have a face-saving effect in that they prepare B for what is going to happen next. For instance, instead of inviting B to a party straightaway A can first make sure that B is free, thus saving B from turning down the <invite> and A from receiving a negative <answer>.

In [197], A makes sure that he is talking to the right person before proceeding:

> [197] A: **but ə you're teaching . ə:m at a GRÁMMAR
> school# ÁREN'T you#**

B: YÈS# *YÈS#*
A: *well* what do you think about SÈX education#
(5.10:382–86)

It would have been possible for A to change the topic, had B's
<answer> been negative. Notice the similarity between a
<preface> and a <question>; they both receive an <answer>. Yet,
what distinguishes the <preface> from the <question> is precisely
that it prepares the way for the <question>.

    <Prefaces> can take a number of shapes, and a list of typical
variants is difficult to present. One variant consists of fixed
expressions such as the following:

   [198] A: **what ÈLSE#** . haven't been up to . WÀLES again
       HÁVE you# . (7.3:741–42)

The function of *what ÈLSE* is fivefold: it arouses B's attention; it
marks a transition between topics; it allows B to come up with a
new topic; it fills a gap in the conversation; and it carries the
conversation forward. Notice that such stereotypes do not require
a [response], although they may occasionally get one.

Summing up opening

Summonsing is used to call the listener's attention to something
new. Focusing may be required by the formality of the situation
or as an introduction to a tricky subject. Framing is used to mark
the transition between stages in the discourse and between topics.

    Notice, however, that a number of exchanges have no
introductory move whatsoever. Nor is there always an explicit
link between the new and the previous exchange.

▶▶▶▶ **Now try this!**

What does A do in the following extracts to introduce the
[initiate]?

   A: well NÓW if this is a FÀCT# . TH=EN# . |i| is it a
       BÓRE# . to go to some other part of the LÍBRARY#
       (3.3:169–73)

   A: what about THÍS# – any GRÁDUATE students here#
       (3.3:456–57)

   A: CHÁIRMAN# may I raise ((a *completely DÌFFERENT))*
       point#

B: *YÈAH#* – TÒTALLY different# *RĬGHT#*

>A: *((we have))* suffered for a long WHĬLE# from the sense of being rather on the FRĬNGE of things# (3.4:754–60)

[Answer on p 214]

Initiating

> The [**initiate**] is the first obligatory move in the exchange

We can initiate an exchange, for instance, by making a <statement>, asking a <question> and putting forward a <request>. And we expect these acts to be replied to, answered, and accepted, respectively. Let's call these the 'basic' initiating acts.

$$[\text{INITIATE}] - \left[\begin{array}{c} \text{<statement>} \\ \text{<question>} \\ \text{<request>} \end{array}\right. - [\text{RESPOND}] - \left[\begin{array}{c} \text{<reply>} \\ \text{<answer>} \\ \text{<answer>} \end{array}\right.$$

♣♣♣ <Commands>, properly speaking, are rare in conversation, and will be dealt with as a kind of <request>.

This looks pretty straightforward. However, there is more than one type of each, and <statements>, <questions> and <requests> as well as their corresponding responding acts will have to be dealt with in terms of subcategories.

Besides, claiming that an exchange can only be initiated by stating, questioning and requesting is clearly simplifying the whole matter. Offering, inviting, thanking and apologizing will be dealt with separately.

Stating

> <**Statements**> supply information and expect to be acknowledged

To 'state' means 'put into words'. It is a very wide concept indeed, but the description will be restricted to two main variants:

$$\langle\text{Statement}\rangle \text{---} \left[\begin{array}{l} \langle\text{inform}\rangle \\ \langle\text{opine}\rangle \end{array} \right.$$

Consider a brief extract from a narrative. A female undergraduate is telling two friends about her visit to a women's college:

> [199] A: I mean I I . the very FÌRST person I met before
> LÚNCH# was |di| əm – – HÌSTORY don# – –
> who was just SWÈET# . you KNÓW# she was ((a
> sort of)) colourless MÒUSE# {of a WÒMAN#}#
> but she was – very SWÈET# and KÌND# and
> PLÈASANT and interesting to TÀLK to# (1.3:
> 959–69)

Is this one long <inform>, is it an <opine>, or is it a combination of both? Obviously a combination. Only the beginning of the extract (*the very FÌRST person I met before LÚNCH# was |ði| əm – – HÌSTORY don#*) is purely informative. All the rest reflects A's opinion of the person she is describing.

However, a distinction between <informs> and <opines> may sometimes be rather difficult to make, as you will probably realize.

<Informs>
<Informs> present neutral information. They are typically realized by a declarative utterance with a falling tone.

An <inform> can be uttered with more or less certainty.

> [200] A: **to tell you the FÂCT#** Malcolm# I couldn't GÉT
> the light# (1.9:1261–62)

Here, *to tell you the FÂCT* emphasizes the truth of the <inform>. A is certain of what he says. At the other end there are cases like:

> [201] A: I heard his name mentioned by – CÀRTER# ((I
> THÍNK))# by DÀRLINGTON# while I was
> DÒWN there# – – – (1.1:585–90)

with *I THÍNK* indicating that the speaker is not at all certain.
Now consider the effect of *you know* and *you see*:

> [202] B: . . . people come in at odd TÌMES# SÒMETIMES
> for ÍNSTANCE# ə this girl who's working at the

> BBC̀# **you see** she has all different SHÌFT
> hours# (5.8:281–84)

[203] A: ÒH# Hart's got this thing about STÀTUS#
YÒU know# he – he doesn't like secretaries to
be merely SÈCRETARIES# (1.5:949–52)

Both *you see* and *YÒU know* serve as <inform> markers, but they
do it differently. *You see* is typically used when A assumes that the
information is new to B. *You know* can be used in the same way
but is more often used when B is either assumed to be somewhat
familiar with the subject already or when A wants to create the
impression that A and B share a common ground.

Moreover, *you know* is often used to hint at some underlying
message. In [203] this is indicated by a somewhat unexpected
intonation contour: *you* and not *know,* carries the tone.

These are some of the most frequent inform markers:

<Inform> markers
actually
as a matter of fact
in fact
the fact is
the point is
you know
you see

♣♣♣ *You know* is generally pronounced in a separate tone unit with
varying intonation contours; *you see* is more often part of a tone
unit, the other items vary

<Opines>

<Opines> express the speaker's personal opinion, his/her feelings
and attitudes. They are generally realized by a declarative and
provided with both lexical and prosodic <opine> markers. The
choice of lexical marker and intonation contour varies with the
attitudes involved:

[204] A: **I TH=INK** to myself# Ì **don't care** whether
they're sort of – particularly DEVÓTED# or NÒT#
. they're so LÓVELY# I THÍNK# (1.12:929–34)

The very beginning, *I TH=INK to myself,* is a clear enough hint.

Moreover, it is *I* that carries the tone and not a word that comes towards the end of the tone unit, which would be the normal case. Finally, *I THINK* emphasizes that this is a question of the speaker's opinion.

What is and what is not a neutral <statement> is usually pretty obvious to conversational partners who share a common ground, even if all explicit verbal (and non-verbal) markers are missing. To the outsider, it might not be altogether obvious.

> **<Opine> markers**
>
> I feel
> I think
> it seems
> it's a pity that
> it's surprising that
> it's . . .

Strategies of highlighting
Making a <statement> is a fairly straightforward thing. However, the speaker may sometimes want to highlight a word or element in the message. Considering that the unmarked focus comes at the end of a unit, the following highlighting strategies are common:

* prefacing
* fronting the focused element
* manipulating the <inform>
* adding an <empathizer>
* adding an <emphasizer>
* adding a <booster>

[205] **prefacing**
A: – – **something I want to go BÁCK to#** – – I acquired an absolutely magnificent SĚWING machine# (1.3: 95–96)

[206] **fronting of focus**
A: **{MǑRGAN} YǑU met#** (2.4:409–11)

[207] **manipulating the <inform>**
A: **and the funny thing ĬS#** that . . . (1.12:936)

[208] A: **what Ǐ like doing is** ə:m . . . (4.3:111)

[209] **adding an <empathizer>**
A: but **you** SÈE# . her TÒOTH fell out# . (4.3:1011–12)

[210] **adding an <emphasizer>**
A: they WÉNT and DÍD it {DÍDN'T they#}# (1.10:3)

Here, the Q-tag could be paraphrased by 'that's what they did'.

[211] **adding a <booster>**
A: *I don't know whether I ever will be ÀBLE to AGÁIN#*
B: *you're having a sabbatical **for God's sake*** . (1.10: 580–81)

In addition, the information in focus can be effectively marked by a particular intonation contour or a pause. Or the <statement> could be turned into a 'rhetorical question' (cf p 94).

▶▶▶▶▶ **Now try this!**

How do you distinguish between an <inform> and an <opine>? What about this utterance, for instance:

A: boards of studies don't . don't DÈAL with RECOGNÍ-TION# this is a − {bloody CÒMPLICATED} UNIVÈR-SITY# (1.2:1012–13)

[Answer on p 214]

Questioning

> <Questions> ask for information or confirmation and expect to be answered

<Questions> can be subclassified according to what kind of <answer> they are asking for:

<Question>──┤ <identification question>
            <polarity question>
            <confirmation question>

[212] <identification question>
A: who do you have for TUTÒRIALS this year#
B: Professor LÙRCH# (6.2:225–26)

[213] <polarity question>
A: locked yourself ÓUT# .
B: YÈS# (1.2:855–56)

[214] <confirmation question>
A: ... ə:m . you can't S=AY# . that . WÓRTH# . is .
ADJECTÌVAL# – RÍGHT#
B: NÒ# – (1.1:651–55)

As we shall see (pp 100–4), all three types of <question> can be used as a cover for other conversational needs, ie as **indirect speech acts**.

<Identification questions>

<Identification questions> ask for an <answer> identifying a *WH*-word

---

<Identification questions> are typically realized by an interrogative sentence containing a *WH*-word. Depending on which *WH*-word is used, the information required is either **specifying** or **open-ended**. *Who, which, where* and *when* ask for specification:

[215] A: **which** is the room NÈXT to it#
B: ə: – the LÈCTURE# SÈMINAR room# (3.3: 937–39)

Only very precise information will do, ie information that 'identifies', or substitutes for, the *WH*-word. If the <question> involves *what, why*, and *how*, on the other hand, there are no restrictions on what kind of information and how much information can be expected. Consider [216]:

[216] A: **how** did you get on at your ÌNTERVIEW# . do TÈLL us#
B: . oh – – – GÒD# what an EXPÈRIENCE# – – – I don't know where to STÀRT# (1.3:215–19)

The <answer> turns into a 20 minutes long and entertaining narrative.
The tone of <identification questions> is typically falling, but it is not always the *WH*-word itself that is placed in the

nuclear position, as [216] demonstrates. When the <question>
asks for clarification concerning the identification of somebody or
something just referred to, on the other hand, the *WH*-word
carries the tone. Then the tone is rising:

> [217] A: ((so)) I SÁID# this just means I shall do half as
>   much WÔRK#((and)) he said . VÈRY well# .
>   B: **WHÓ said this#**
>   A: the SÈCRETARY# . of the SCHÒOL# (2.4:
>   378–83)

The same refers to **echo-questions**, so called because they repeat
part of what the previous speaker said:

> [218] A: and I can't get back to bloody BRǓGES# for a nine
>   o'clock . *((and I))*
>   B: ***you can't get* back to WHÁT#**
>   A: to BRǓGES# (8.4:692–95)

Echo-questions resemble <checks> (pp 39–41) in that they make
the previous speaker repeat (part of) what he just said. In other
cases they express strong surprise and resemble <reacts>.

<Identification questions> should be kept separate from so-
called **rhetorical questions** which are also generally expressed
by a *WH*-interrogative:

> [219] A: {WHÝ} SHÒULD somebody MÓVE {HÉRE#}#
>   . when he has to pay FÍFTY thousand PÓUNDS#
>   or thirty thousand pounds for a HÒUSE# –
>   (11.2:457–59)

This 'question' can be paraphrased by 'of course nobody wants to
move here' and is equivalent to a forceful <statement>.

Quite frequently <identification questions> appear in the
shape of so-called 'alternative questions', ie an interrogative
presenting two (or more) alternatives to choose from:

> [220] A: ə: shall I come ÉARLIER# **or at four O'CLÒCK#**
>   B: no I should CÒME at {four o'CLÒCK#}#
>   (7.2:167–69)

This is a matter of 'when'; A's utterance can be paraphrased by
'when do you want me to come.'

> [221] A: ə:m is it a matter of . what the money ÍS# – or
>   the kind of WÓRK# or WHÀT# .

B: WÈLL# it's {RÈALLY sort of} what the MÒNEY
is# (3.2:281–84)

Here, it is a matter of 'what'.

The first alternative typically carries a rising tone, the second
a falling tone. Given the appropriate situation, it might even be
possible to use a declarative utterance with a rising tone:

[222] A: you're rushing ÓFF# – –
B: I was THÌNKING# that if I GÒ# . I might get into
SÀINSBURY'S {before they CLÒSE#}# . (1.8:
279–82)

Judging by the <answer>, this is obviously a matter of 'why'.

<Polarity questions>

<Polarity questions> ask for a *yes/no* <answer>

<Polarity questions> are typically realized by an utterance
involving inverted word-order:

[223] A: are you available during DĂYLIGHT hours# (8.1:
1209)

or *do*-periphrasis:

[224] A: do you know Malcolm BŎWEN# over at the
COMPÙTER ÚNIT# (1.6:24–25)

The tone is typically rising, which means that the utterance is
marked for <question> function both syntactically and prosodically. In addition, there may of course be lexical clues. Nothing
in the form of the <question> indicates that the questioner
expects *yes* rather than *no* or vice versa. In that respect the
<answer> is open-ended.

If the speaker assumes that such and such is the case, on the
other hand, s/he might use a declarative sentence:

[225] A: there's a CASSÉTTE {GÓES with that#}# . (3.2:868)

A falling tone would be even more indicative of the questioner's
assumption.

Like <identification questions>, <polarity questions> can
take the form of 'alternative questions':

[226] A: ə: if you were to buy a house that was BĬG

enough# would you take {ÌN} any tenants **or** NÒT# .

B: NÒ# (8.2:286–87)

In fact, <polarity questions> can be regarded as curtailed alternative questions with only one – the first – alternative spelt out.

<*Confirmation questions*>

> **<Confirmation questions>** ask for a confirming <answer>

<Confirmation questions> are typically realized by a declarative utterance and a tag (*aren't you, doesn't it*, etc), a so-called 'tag-question'. What is to be confirmed is expressed in the declarative part, usually with a falling tone, and the request for confirmation is expressed in the tag, generally with a rising tone inviting confirmation:

[227] A: she had a RÈST# . DÍDN'T she# (11.1:714–15)

But tones vary, depending on the speaker's expectations.

The normal thing is that the tag occupies a separate tone unit. This is one exception:

[228] A: Thorpe's AWÁY **is he**# (1.6:186)

equivalent to 'I gather that Thorpe's away'. On certain occasions a simple declarative will do. [229] is from a legal cross-examination, where counsel deliberately evokes a <confirm>:

[229] A: she was sitting ÙP in BÉD# (11.1:1026)

Sometimes, what looks like a <confirmation question> is used as an <opine>. Take the following, for instance:

[230] A: this ((I think)) PRÒVES# that . ((that's)) a rather
weak CHÁRACTER# **DÒESN'T it**#

B: MÁYBE# (1.6:443–46)

which could be paraphrased by 'don't you agree with me that that's a rather weak character'.

What we generally mean by a tag is a string consisting of an auxiliary verb and a pronoun with or without *not*, which is added to a declarative. But there are variants; *OK*, *right*, and *alright* are the most obvious candidates.

```
┌─────────────────────────────────────────┐
│  Tags                                    │
│                                          │
│  aux + pron ± not: is(n't) he            │
│                    does(n't) she         │
│                    has(n't) it           │
│                    etc                   │
│  ALRÍGHT, OK̗, RÍGHT                      │
└─────────────────────────────────────────┘
```

♣♣♣ The tone of the tag varies (and may even be lacking)

How <questions> are recognized
The three types of <question> described above can be recognized
by the following criteria:

Features	Type of <question>		
	<Q:ident>	<Q:polar>	<Q:conf>
SYNTAX			
inversion		+	
do-periphrasis	+/−	+	
declarative ± tag			+
alternative	+	+	
INTONATION			
fall	+	(+)	+
rise	(+)	+	+
LEXIS			
WH-word	+		
Q-word	+	+	+

♣♣♣ Typical Q-words are the adverbs *perhaps* and *probably* and the
verbs *assume*, *guess* and *suppose*

As we have seen, it should neither be taken for granted that
all interrogative utterances can be interpreted as <questions>, nor
that <questions> cannot take other than interrogative form. What
finally decides the function of an utterance is the actual speech
situation, including the speakers' shared knowledge. A declarative
utterance with a falling tone, for instance, which usually functions
as an <inform>, will automatically become a <question> if it is
uttered by A and contains information that only B knows:

[231] A: I don't think there's enough MÒNEY in the
department {to SPÈND#}# .
B: (– breathes) **this is the money for the buying
of BÒOKS#**
A: YÈS# (3.3:403–05)

What B says may be paraphrased by 'do you mean the
money for the buying of books'; B cannot really know what
money A is talking about.

Highlighting questions
In the simple case A asks a straightforward <question> and waits
for B to answer. In other cases a more complex procedure may
be used, eg:

* fronting the Q-element
* manipulating the Q-act

Fronting the Q-element
The word that the questioner wishes to place in focus, is 'lifted'
from its ordinary position in the <question> to first position in
the utterance and the gap is filled by a substitute, here a pronoun:

[232] A: **this P=OLLY#** ... do you KNÓW her# (1.4:
887–97)

Manipulating the Q-act
Sometimes the <question> is introduced by a <precursor>, which
links up with what was said before, or followed by a <clue>,
which provides additional information. Compare the following
extracts from a discussion about university studies and academic
teaching. A has just mentioned one of her favourite lecturers:

[233] **<precursor>**
A: **he's a very GÒOD lecturer#**
have you ever HÉARD him# –
B: no I H=AVEN'T# . (1.6:746–48)

[234] **<clue>**
A: did did you {GÒ} to HÌS lectures#
they were very DRÝ and# very AMÙSING# .
(5.9:951–53)

Additions of this kind may not be necessary for the understanding
but they certainly add to the social aspect of the conversation.

From the point of view of content, the <clue> comments on the <question> in the same initiating move, while the <precursor> comments on something in the preceding dialogue.

Generally, <clues> are either intended to help B answer the <question> by providing additional information or by reformulating the <question>, or they reflect what A expects B to say:

[235] A: . . . where did you hear THÀT#
you must have coined ((this)) **YOURSÈLF#**
(1.1:529–30)

Another way of manipulating the <question> is by reformulating it. The effect of this is generally that the reformulation and not the original <question> is the one that is answered:

[236] A: but what made you DECÌDE# –
did you did you go from UNIVÈRSITY# |s| **to**
SECRETÀRIAL school#
B: YÈS# (5.9:294–97)

[237] A: **how's all the TUTÒRIAL side#** – – – ə:
departmental TÚTOR side# is THÁT all right#
B: =M# (3.3:1057–60)

The long silent pause after A's first <question> indicates that he expects B to answer. The fact that she does not and that A has to ask a second <question>, which explains the first, turns the first one into a <preface>, while the second elicits the <answer>.

WHAT <questions> are USED FOR

* to get information/confirmation
* to create contact
* to start and carry on a conversation
* to ask permission to do something
* to get somebody to do something

Requesting

<Requests> ask B to do something or to let A do something and expect to be accepted

There are two categories of request, as the definition suggests:

<Request>——⌈ <action request>
⌊ <permission request>

♣♣♣ Remember that <commands> are included in the <request>
category

<Action requests> ask somebody to do something

[238] A: **could you give me another RECOMMENDA-**
TION#
B: oh YÈS# (6.2:309–10)

<Permission requests> ask for a go-ahead

[239] A: **can I SMÒKE in here *|dei| . DÁVID*#**
B: *PLÈASE# PLÈASE* old fellow# (5.11:2–4)

The fact that both categories can be answered by *yes* or *no* seems
to indicate that they are basically <polarity questions>. Indeed,
what decides the interpretation is only the actual situation. This is
perhaps most obvious with respect to *can I SMÒKE in here*, which
could either ask whether it is possible to smoke or whether one is
allowed to smoke. By contrast, *could you give me another*
RECOMMENDÀTION would probably be interpreted as asking for
action in the first place, since *could you* is a conventional marker
of <request> function.

How <requests> are made
Both types of <request> are realized by interrogative, declarative
and imperative utterances.

<Action requests>

Interrogative could you give an EXÀMPLE# (1.3:969)
Declarative I want you to get back as quickly as you
CÀN# (4.2:978)
Imperative GÌVE it to him# (2.10:288)

<Permission requests>

Interrogative may I read your MĚSSAGE# (1.8:376)

Declarative I would like if I MÁY# to turn to two
PÒINTS# (5.6:911–12)
Imperative let me FÌNISH# (5.3:649)

A <request> can be more or less polite and more or less
urgent. In either case, the choice of grammatical form and lexical
content, in combination with intonation pattern, is likely to have
an impact. For instance, the imperative 'BELÌEVE me' is likely to
be perceived as less urgent than:

[240] A: oh yes **do do** BELÌEVE me# . (5.4:799)

And 'hold ÒN' would definitely be less polite than:

[241] A: hold =ON . **PLÉASE#** . (7.2:1333)

The conventional, polite way of expressing a <request>
consists in using an interrogative, preferably with the addition of
please. The least polite form would be a plain imperative. Yet, an
urgent situation might trigger off an imperative without
necessarily being perceived as impolite.

Making a <request> requires tact and caution; neither party
can afford to lose face. Therefore, <requests> are often preceded
by a <preface>, where A makes sure that certain pre-conditions
hold before making the <request>:

[242] A: **but ə you're teaching at . ə:m at a GRÀM-**
MAR school# ÀREN'T you#
B: YÈS# *YÈS#*
A: *well* what do you think about SÈX education# .
(5.10:382–86)

Another face-saving strategy is to add a <justify> explaining
why the <request> is made:

[243] A: have you got a PÉN# **I'll leave a MÈSSAGE#**
(1.8:360–61)

Notice that in neither case does the interrogative contain a
<request> marker, but it is still fairly evident that both [242] and
[243] are intended as <action requests>.

Some <action requests> are expressed by means of *I think* (eg
'I think you should . . .' and *I suggest* (eg 'I suggest you . . .').
These are not always easy to distinguish from <opines> and
<suggests>.

▶▶▶▶▶ **Now try this!**

The following <requests> occurred in telephone calls.

[a] Try to order them from 'most polite' to 'least polite':

A: do you KNŎW the ADDRÉSS# (8.2:971)

A: would you TĚLL him# (7.3:43)

A: could you give her a MĔSSAGE for me# (8.1:862)

A: ə:m . is she THĚRE please# (8.2:1039)

A: can you ĂSK her to ring her SOLĬCITORS# –
     (9.1:287)

A: how about somebody giving MÈ a game# (11.3:
     543)

A: I wonder if you could put me on your MÂILING-LIST
     please (8.2:3)

A: will you pass that ÓN to him# (7.3:13)

[b] What difficulties are involved?

[Suggested answer on p 214]

Summing up stating, questioning and requesting

The three basic strategies used to initiate an exchange are:

• stating
• questioning
• requesting

Other strategies are offering, inviting, apologizing and thanking.
Each of the basic strategies is carried out by means of a corresponding set of acts:

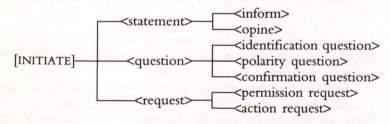

♣♣♣ <Commands> are included in <requests>

As regards form, <identification questions> are generally, but not always, realized by a *WH*-interrogative, <polarity questions> by inversion, and <confirmation questions> by a declarative plus tag.

Various procedures are used to highlight the 'core' of the question, such as fronting, framing, focusing and prefacing. The way the act is expressed is particularly important when it comes to <requests>, and also <offers> and <invites>.

▶▶▶▶ **Now try this!**

It is obvious that the choice of form plays quite an important role for the type of <question> we want to express and also that the interpretation relies heavily on the context. How do you interpret the part of the following utterances that is printed in boldface?

[a] A: has Jock TŎLD you all this# **I'm not just WÀSTING my TÍME#**

B: no NÒ# (3.2:194–96)

[b] A: I'm not being funny about her STÂYING THŎUGH# . because you KNÒW# I M=EAN# **how many people have STÀYED with us#** – – (– – laughs) thousand and ÔNE# (4.1:978–82)

[Suggested answer on p 215]

Other initiating acts

Stating, questioning and requesting are not the only initiating strategies. Let's consider a few others:
* offering and inviting
* apologizing
* thanking

Offering and inviting

<Offers> and <invites> submit something for acceptance

Although <offer> and <invites> can be defined roughly in the same way, they are not doing exactly the same thing in the interaction. Compare [244] and [245]:

> [244] <offer>
> A: would you like one of THŎSE#
> B: yes PLÉASE# (2.12:316– 17)

> [245] A: you ought to come over to CÁMBRIDGE some-
>   time# . have a look RÒUND#
>   B: M̂# . (4.5:29– 32)

They are both intended to benefit B, but whereas the <offer> is costly to A, the <invite> does not have to be. In [244], for instance, A offers to give something away 'unrewarded', but in [245] A may like the thought of having B around.

How <offers> and <invites> are made
<Offers> and <invites> are realized in the same way as <requests>, namely by interrogative, declarative and imperative utterances.

<Offers>

Interrogative	want any SÚGAR# (1.8:43)
Declarative	I'll buy you a cup of TÉA# (2.7:793)
Imperative	have a glass of SHÉRRY# (1.2:844)

<Invites>

Interrogative	won't you sit down (3.1:10)
Declarative	now is the time for all good men to come to the aid of the PÀRTY# (7.2:11)
Imperative	pop in and SÈE me# (7.1:1095)

The randomly picked examples reflect a fairly high degree of casualness. Formality seems to play a less important role when offering and inviting than it does when requesting, maybe because the face-saving aspect is a less vital issue. This is partly an illusion, however, one reason being that the speakers in the above extracts happen to know each other well, another that the actual situations invite casualness.

Clearly, there are situations where polite forms are important, just as there are situations where the offerer/inviter has to make sure that necessary pre-conditions hold so that a <reject>

is avoided. By and large, however, the freedom of choice seems to be larger for <offers> and <invites> than for <requests>.

Apologizing

> **<Apologies>** ask for forgiveness

<Apologies> are like <action requests> in that they ask B to do something, but as far as the cost/benefit dichotomy is concerned they are different:

[246] A: HELLÓ# . **sorry I'm LÁTE#**
b: (. laughs) that's alright are you – (2.7:2–4)

This is apparently a minor offense. Still, it may cost A some pride to apologize. On the other hand she benefits from being forgiven, and the way the <apology> is received and responded to clearly reveals that 'forgiving' does not cost b anything.

A <justify> may be added as an explanation:

[247] A: I'm sorry I was LÁTE# .   <apology>
my train . didn't ARRÌVE# –   <justify>
(2.11:534–35)

An <apology> can be formulated in a number of ways, depending on the circumstances. This is the 'meeting version':

[248] A: CHǍIRMAN# . **EXCÙSE me#** could I ÀDD that
əm – . . . (5.13:137–39)

This 'apology' was not responded to for obvious reasons. For [responses] to <apologies>, see pp 120–1.

> **<Apologies>**
>
> scuse me
> excuse me
> forgive me
> sorry
> I'm sorry
> I'm terribly sorry
> I beg your pardon

♣♣♣ 'Polite' <apologies> generally have a falling tone
'Deeply felt' <apologies> generally have a falling-rising tone

Thanking

<Thanks> express gratitude

<Thanks> can act both as an [initiate] and as a [response] (cf pp 121–2).

[249] A: *thanks very MÚCH#*
B: *THÀNK you# . * (8.2:1244–45)

Above all, <thanks> is a politeness device, which can be used conveniently to terminate a conversation. The most frequent realizations of <thanks> in the Corpus are *thank you*, *thanks*, and *thanks very much*, in that order.

<Thanks>

thanks
thanks a lot
thanks awfully
thanks very much
thanks very much indeed
thank you
thank you so much
thank you very much
thank you very much indeed

♣♣♣ the tone is usually falling

Repairing

Repairing involves clearing up before proceeding

What A says may be inaudible, incomprehensible or hard to believe, and B may have to ask for repetition, clarification or confirmation. The resulting [repair]-[response] sequence causes a momentary interruption but is necessary for the completion of the exchange and for the conversation to go on.

One act that often triggers off a [repair] sequence is the

<request>. If A asks B to do something, B might want to know the reason why before accepting, or s/he might simply need more information in order to carry out the action, as in [250] where B is asked to look for a file:

[250] A: . . . the BRÒWN one# . it's got a {NÙMBER} on the FRÒNT# . could you LÒOK on it# and tell me what the NÙMBER is# .
B: the number on the FRÒNT# . **where did you LÉAVE the file#**
A: **it's on top of the TÝPEWRITER# or BÝ the typewriter#**
B: . . . ((I'll just LÒOK))# – – (7.3:991–1000)

Likewise, if A asks permission to do something, B might want to know why before giving her/his permission. In addition, the [repair] sequence can serve very conveniently as a filler for time.

Checking

<Checks> ask for repetition and clarification

<Checks> are realized by such items as *what, sorry, pardon,* and *I beg your pardon,* and by interrogative words (*WH*-words) and utterances:

[251] **asking for repetition**
A: you know the SÁFEST CONTRACÉPTIVE {DÓ you#}#
B: NÓ#
A: ((the)) two phonemic CLÙSTER# . NÒ# .
⌈ B: **WHÁT# WHÁT was that again#**
⌊ A: the two {PHONÉMIC} . CLÙSTER# . NÒ#
(– – – laughs)
B: *(– – – laughs)* (1.1:520–29)

The play with words would have got completely lost if A had not been asked to repeat it. The way B does it, adding *WHÁT was that again* instead of restricting himself to a simple *WHÁT* or *SÓRRY,* seems to indicate that he is eager to have the words repeated. Not much distinguishes this <check> from an echo-question (p 94); it is a matter of degree.

[252] **asking for clarification**

> A: even the local AUTHŌRITY# had refused ((a *MÒRT-
> *GAGE on it))#
>> B: *WHȲ* – #
>> A: because it was so clapped ÒUT#
> B: YÈAH# (4.2:308–12)

B has no difficulty in hearing or understanding what A says. She
is only curious to know the reason for refusing a mortgage. WHȲ
seems to be uttered somewhat prematurely, however. Apparently,
A had already decided to go on and explain what he meant,
something that B could hardly have anticipated.

The degree of politeness in terms of lexical choice varies
with the situation. A simple WHÁT, for instance, in a friendly chat
might be felt as more appropriate than I beg your PÁRDON.

```
<Checks>

I beg your pardon
I'm sorry
pardon
sorry
what
when, where, who, why
```

♣♣♣ <Checks> asking for repetition generally carry a rising tone;
<checks> asking for clarification tend to have a falling tone,
unless they signal surprise

Summing up repairing

[Repair] sequences are embedded in and therefore subordinate
to the main exchange. [Repairs] are realized by <checks> which
ask for repetition or clarification of what was said in the
immediately preceding turn. The main exchange cannot be
completed until the <check> has been responded to.

▶▶▶▶▶ **Now try this!**

The following extract is not considered to contain a [repair]
sequence. Can you figure out why? I shall give you a lead.
Compare elliptical coupling (p 53).

> A: well I PREFĔR# Lord of the FLÌES# – –

B: WHY# − −

A: because I don't think I UNDERSTOOD Pincher MARTIN# (3.1:399–402)

[Answer on p 215]

Responding

> <The [**response**] is B's next obligatory move in the exchange after A's [initiate]

The 'basic' initiating acts and their corresponding responding acts are repeated here for the sake of convenience:

$$
[\text{INITIATE}] - \left[\begin{array}{c} \text{<statement>} \\ \text{<question>} \\ \text{<request>} \end{array} \right] - [\text{RESPOND}] - \left[\begin{array}{c} \text{<reply>} \\ \text{<answer>} \\ \text{<answer>} \end{array} \right]
$$

The [response] can consist of anything from a minimal receipt of information, an <acknowledge>, to a long and exhaustive <answer> to a <question>.

[253] **acknowledging a <statement>**

A: . . . but it seemed the only thing to SAY# she was in such a MESS#

B: M# (5.8:107–09)

[254] **answering a <question>**

B: − − how did you get on at your INTERVIEW# . do TELL us#

A: **. oh − − GOD# what an EXPERIENCE# − − I don't know where to START# you KNOW# it was just such a NIGHTMARE# − − I mean this whole SYSTEM#** . . . (1.3:215–222)

The way we respond is a result of what was done in the initiating move. If the previous speaker made a <statement>, we respond by a <reply>; if s/he asked a <question>, we respond by an <answer>; if s/he made a <request>, we respond by an <answer>.

Responding to <statements>

When we make a <statement>, we expect a <reply> signalling some kind of reaction. Three subcategories of the <reply> have been identified:

$$\text{<Reply>} \left\{ \begin{array}{l} \text{<acknowledge>} \\ \text{<agree>} \\ \text{<object>} \end{array} \right.$$

A <reply> to a <statement> containing mere facts is likely to be different from a <reply> to a <statement> reflecting the speaker's personal opinion.

Acknowledging <informs> and <opines>

> **<Acknowledges>** signal that B accepts what A said as a valid contribution to the conversation

When A informs B of something, B is expected to show that s/he has received the information. The most economical way of responding is using an <acknowledge>, which is an extremely useful device, since it allows B to respond without revealing whether s/he approves or disapproves of what s/he heard. It may also reflect B's attitude to what A said, more or less strongly. B's degree of involvement, ranging from mere acceptance (or maybe concealed disapproval) to strong (or maybe faked) surprise, is reflected not only in the choice of lexical item and the combination of items but also in the intonation contour. Examples [255] to [257] are ordered from least to most involved (cf [backchannels] p 82):

[255] A: he wants to get on with his Estonian ((ABORÌGI-
          NAL))#
       B: =M# – (1.2:1149–50)

[256] A: Ì haven't got any MÁRKS#
       B: ÒH# – (4.2:953–54)

[257] A: I have |də| no NÈWS of WĚSSEX# at ÀLL#
       B: |r| REÀLLY# (8.4:1062–64)

[258] is reinforced by a <booster>:

[258] A: well I STÀRT at ÉIGHT#
       B: m M̀# HÉLL# – PÓOR YOU# – (2.5:170–73)

<Opines> can of course also be merely acknowledged:

[259] A: ... I mean he's a very {ÌNTERESTING} CÁN-
DIDATE HÉRMAN I think# although he HÉ'S
becoming ÓLD# about THIRTY-FÓUR#
B: =M . (2.6:757–61)

But often, a mere <acknowledge> is felt to be insufficient,
and it is often followed by an <expand>, where B comments on
or objects to the information provided by A:

[260] A: I MÈT him ÓNCE# at a DÌNNER# – *in the*
MÙSIC *((hall))#*
B: YÈAH#   he(('s))   *((was   in))   a*   –
BÁLLET critic# ah MÙSIC# . ((no BÀL-
LET))# he was BÀLLET# (1.4:1066–73)

<Acknowledges>

ah	really
all right	right
I see	goodness
oh	gosh
OK	oh dear
quite	

♣♣♣ The tone is usually falling, sometimes rising-falling. Many items
used as <acknowledges> can realize other acts

Agreeing to <informs> and <opines>

<Agrees> indicate that B approves of what A means

If A just provides information, there is no need for B to do more
than approve and let A go on:

[261] A: ... I'm seeing if Methuen will stump up any
MÒNEY# to cover the man's TÌME#
B: GÒOD# – – – (1.8:243–45)

However, for the conversation to run smoothly, a one-word
<agree> eg realized by *good* or *fine*, may be felt to be insufficient
and some kind of addition may be needed. Since conversation is a
continuous give and take, B often acknowledges receipt of

information and goes on (cf <uptakes> pp 46–7). B is generally quite willing to contribute his own piece of information or opinion:

[262] A: and they were NAÏVE ENÓUGH# to . *be taken
     ÌN ((by it))#*
    B: * – YÈS#* **this is the funny thing ABÒUT
     academics#** – . (1.6:343–46)

It may not be surprising that neutral information is usually not objected to, but even <opines> are remarkably often followed by a [response] reflecting complete agreement:

[263] A: that chap from PLÁYDEN# should(('ve)) NÈVER
     have spoken# at ÂLL# *NÒ# M̂*
    B: ***Mr RÒBBY#** {**YÈS#**}#* ((which)) kept saying
     my name is RÒBEY (– – – laughs) I now call upon
     Mr RÒBBY {to SPÈAK#}# my name's RÒBEY# (–
     – laughs) – **yes he was COMPLÈTELY mad#**
     (2.8:826–35)

<Agrees>	
absolutely	precisely
all right	quite
fine	right
good	that's right
OK	yes (no)

♣♣♣ The tone is usually falling or rising-falling

Objecting to <informs> and <opines>

<Objects> signal that B does not agree with A

It would be odd, to say the least, if B agreed to everything A said. It would either give the impression that B did not have an opinion of her/his own, or that s/he either did not have anything to say or was simply not interested, with disastrous consequences for the conversation.

Objecting requires a certain level of politeness. This is why <objects> tend to be introduced by an <uptake>, for instance realized by *oh*, *well*, and *yes* (or *no* in case of a preceding negative utterance), all with a shock-absorbing effect. When it comes to *yes* (and *no*), it seems as if B agrees before s/he makes clear that s/he does not:

[264] A: I always thought they got on WÈLL TOGÉTHER#
both have strong WĬLLS#
B: **yes but** MILÓRD# . əm strong-willed PÉOPLE#
have to TÁKE# . one another for better or
WÓRSE# the same as people WITHÒUT strong
{WĬLLS#}# (12.3:1063–69)

[265] A: he knew nothing of concrete and GLÀSS# – –
B: NÒ# . **but** he would have been QÚITE good# at
doing THÀT I THÍNK# (4.4:458–60)

Yes [264] could be paraphrased by 'I see what you mean', and *no*
[265] by 'I quite agree as far as that is concerned'.

Well is different; it always signals hesitation, or doubt, or
scepticism, and so on. With *well* it is immediately obvious that B
does not share A's opinion altogether:

[266] A: . . . there's no RÈASON# why it should be so
surprising#
B: **well but** they were SURPRÍSED#
A: oh THÉY were surprised# YÉS# (2.8:589–92)

▶▶▶▶▶ **Now try this!**

What does B contribute to the dialogue?

A: I'm {THÍNKING of CLÀIMING {for my Whitaker's
ÁLMANACK#}# –
B: M̌# –
A: I've put in a CHÈCK {CL=AIM#}# for twenty-one
pound – – ÒDD# –
B: =M̌# – (4.1:337–41)

[Answer on p 215]

Responding to <questions>

A <question> expects a proper <answer>. The following are
proper <answers> to <identification questions>, <polar ques-
tions> and <confirmation questions>.

[267] **<identification question>**
A: where have they moved to NÒW#
B: into QUÈEN Street# (5.9:786–87)

[268] **<polar question>**
A: did you know that DÒRNHOPE# was master of
HÙSTLEFORD#
B: YÈS# (5.9:121–23)

[269] **<confirmation question>**
A: ə:m ə: see you next WÈEK no doubt#
B: YÈS# Ì'll be ÍN# – – – (1.8:389–91)

But not all <answers> are 'proper' in the sense that they
really **answer** the <question>. The following subcategories can
occur, ordered from most to least appropriate:

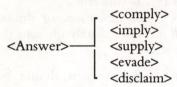

<Answer>
- <comply>
- <imply>
- <supply>
- <evade>
- <disclaim>

Only <complies> are proper in that they answer a <question>
directly and adequately; all the others are not exactly or not at all
'to the point'. Compare the examples below, and you will see the
difference.

Complying

[270] **<comply>**
A: WHÉN is it#
B: four THÌRTY {TOMÒRROW#}# (1.4:1118–19)

The <comply> *four THÌRTY TOMÒRROW* provides no more
and no less than the information asked for. In other words, it
answers the <question> directly.

Implying

[271] **<imply>**
A: do you want people to come to the RĚGISTRY office# –
B: not MÀNY# (7.3:785–86)

It is possible to infer the direct <answer> from the <imply> *not
MÀNY*, something like 'yes I do but not too many'; it answers
the <question> indirectly.

Supplying

[272] **<supply>**
A: was he a personal FRÌEND of YÓURS or# .
B: əm . well . ə . he used to be my tutor (5.9:79–80)

B does not really answer the <question>, since he does not make clear whether 'he' was a personal friend as well as tutor. The information is beside the point. Such <answers> are typically introduced by *well*, often in combination with pauses, as in this example.

Evading

[273] **<evade>**
A: ə:m well have you any ÓTHER {SUGGÉSTIONS#}# .
B: well he didn't GÌVE me any# (8.2:1105–06)

Rather than admitting that she cannot suggest anything B refers to a third party who is not present. Doing so, she avoids answering 'no'. Notice again the use of *well*.

Disclaiming

[274] **<disclaim>**
A: what happens if anybody breaks in and STĚALS it# – are are is are we CÓVERED# or
B: ə:m – I don't KNÒW quite HÓNESTLY# . (1.8:418–21)

After a moment of hesitation, B comes up with an <answer> that is honest and straightforward but which does not answer the <question> and does not pretend to do so.

the **<comply>**	gives adequate information explicitly
the **<imply>**	gives adequate information implicitly
the **<supply>**	gives inadequate information
the **<evade>**	avoids answering (consciously)
the **<disclaim>**	declares that the <answer> is unknown

▶▶▶▶▶ **Now try this!**

[a] What type of <answer> does B give?
A: has Ivor gone HÓME# –
B: ((I)) THÌNK so# (4.1:1013–14)

[b] Use the same <question> and try to provide the other four <answer> types. They have all been defined and exemplified above.

[Answer on p 215]

Responding to <requests>

The following subcategories of <replies> to <requests> have been identified:

$$\text{<Reply>} \longrightarrow \begin{cases} \text{<accept>} \\ \text{<evade>} \\ \text{<reject>} \end{cases}$$

<Requests> are face-threatening acts for two reasons. First, they are costly to B and benefitting to A and second, they are open to rejections. Accepting, being a positive action, is no big problem. It is rejecting that often requires both tact and diplomacy.

Accepting

[275] **<action request>**
A: and ((also)) could you get some CHÈESE please# –
B: I'll GÈT some# . YÉS# . (7.2:525–27)

YÉS would have been a fully satisfactory <answer>; it is added for emphasis, it seems.

[276] **<permission request>**
A: can I pinch a CÍGGIE#
B: CÒURSE you can# (2.11:285–86)

The <request> is not only casual but slangy. No wonder the <accept> is informal. The speakers are two young colleagues, which explains the informal style.

Evading

[277] A: could you SĔE what's still to come Fanny# cos I think they . there are {TWÒ performances} of each ÒNE# – . . .
B: **trouble is I don't RÉGULARLY have a PÀPER#** it doesn't get DELÌVERED# so I sometimes BÙY one and . . . (2.5:1167–81)

B wants very much to carry out what she is asked to do but is unable to for obvious reasons. She does not say so in plain words, however; instead she provides 'the reason why'.

Rejecting

The two situations that the following extracts are taken from are very different. [278] is from the husband-wife dialogue, [279] from a telephone call to a university department:

[278] <action request>
A: can you pick your own TRÒUSERS up# .
B: **NÒ# – I don't think it'll |?| LÌKELY# I've got this
. meeting at three THÌRTY#** – – – (4.1:9–12)

[279] <action request>
A: is Mrs DÁVY there please# .
B: **SÓRRY# she's ÌNTERVIEWING this morning#** (9.1:
700–02)

But although the <reject> in [279] is definitely more polite than the one in [278] the two extracts have one thing in common. In both cases the <reject> is followed by a <justify> giving the reason why. This is an almost obligatory addition; without it, the speaker risks being rude.

▶▶▶▶ **Now try this!**

These occurred as <accepts> to <action requests>. Could any of them be used to answer <permission requests>?

B: ÒK#
B: I'll TRỲ to#
B: RÍGHT# I WÌLL#
B: ÒK#
B: CÉRTAINLY#

[Answer on p 216]

Summing up responding to <statements>, <questions> and <requests>

The way the basic initiating moves are responded to has been described in the following terms:

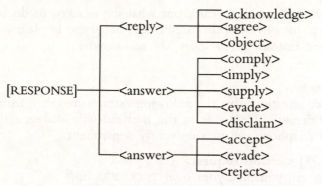

When replying to a <statement> the respondent has to make a decision; is s/he just going to acknowledge receipt of information, or agree to or object to what was said.

Proper <answers> to <questions> require knowledge but, as we have seen, it is possible to respond without knowing the proper <answer>. <Confirmation questions> are of course considerably easier to get away with than the rest; if the answerer does not know whether it is 'yes' or 'no', s/he can just confirm the respondent's assumption.

<Answers> to <requests>, <offers> and <invites> require tact. These are potential face-threatening acts.

Responding to <apologies> and <thanks>, finally, requires a certain degree of politeness.

Responding to <offers> and <invites>

<Offers> and <invites> are the opposites of <requests> insofar as it is B and not A who benefits from the proposed action, which is more or less costly to A. Yet, the act of rejecting may be just as problematic and may require just as much tact as when it comes to rejecting <requests>.

<Answer>———⎡ <accept>
⎢ <evade>
⎣ <reject>

Accepting
[280] **<offer>**
A: D=AN# can I not get you a DRÌNK#
B: **yes you MÀY# THÀNK you#** (4.4:855–57)

A male teacher in his late twenties is visiting a couple of friends of

the same age. The wording of the <accept> is somewhat
unexpected. Why *you MÀY* and *not 'yes please'*? Perhaps it is
triggered off by *not* in the <offer>. Or it could be ironical or have
some other reason that is perfectly clear to the parties involved.

[281] <invite>
A: would you like to take some LÙNCH . *young
PÁULINE#*
B: *M̀# . ((that would))* be very NÌCE PLÉASE# – (6.2:
1038–40)

This sequence occurs in a private conversation between a 40-year
old male academic and a 25-year old ex-student. Although the
<invite> seems to be made half jokingly, the <accept> is perfectly
polite and 'ordinary'.

Evading
[282] <invite>
A: when are you coming to SÈE us then#
b: ə:m –
A: can you get down before Dan has the BÁBY#
b: I think we might manage it ə:m – – it's ə you
know things are a bit hectic but ə:m – ə: . . .
(7.1:489–92)

Notice the hesitation, *I think we might, you know . . . but* and the
filled pauses, before b goes on to explain how tired his wife gets
from travelling.

Rejecting
[283] <offer>
A: what about a CIGARÈTTE# . *((4 sylls))*
B: *I WÒN'T have one THÁNKS# (1.8:147–49)

Two colleagues are having a chat. The <offer> is very casual. No
wonder the <reject> is also somewhat casual.

[284] <invite>
A: now is the time for all good men to come to the aid of
the PÀRTY#
B: YÈS# (. laughs) I'm afraid I'm just laid ÙP# I
don't know what it ÌS# I think it's the FLÚ#
(7.2:11–15)

This exchange is from a telephone call. A female researcher is inviting a somewhat younger postgraduate student to a party. There is no doubt that B appreciates the cheerful tone of the <invite>. He avoids a direct *no* and restricts himself to giving a 'reason why' he cannot come.

As you may have noticed, the form of both <accepts> and <rejects>, besides reflecting the 'style' of the previous act, is very much a matter of speaker relations, what the <offer> and <invite> involve, and how they are expressed.

▶▶▶▶▶ **Now try this!**

Suggest possible ways of accepting, evading and rejecting the following <offer>:

A: have a glass of SHÉRRY# . (1.2:844)

[Suggested answer p 216]

Responding to <apologies>

Responding to an <apology> is mainly a matter of being polite. Compare the following:

[285] A: SÒRRY to bother you#   <apology>
     B: **NÒ# not a BÌT#** . (8.4:536–38)   <smoother>

A female researcher apologizes for asking a male adminstrator to send her an article.

[286] A: . . . SÒRRY about THÍS Ralph# *I .
     B: ***don't WÓRRY#** . (5.11:16–18)

Two colleagues are having a private conversation, when the telephone rings. Speaker A feels obliged to answer while B is sitting there waiting for him to finish. When the phone-call is over A apologizes.

[287] A: SÒRRY to be a BÓRE#
     B: **you're not a bore a BÍT#** (7.2:1372–73)

This is from a telephone talk between two female colleagues. A apologizes for not being able to take part in meeting as agreed on earlier.

The reasons for apologizing are trivial, and the wording of the <apologies> is informal in all three cases. They are consequently responded to in a fairly casual way.

[Responses] to <apologies> mirror the reason for apologizing, who apologizes, the actual situation and the way the <apology> was expressed.

▶▶▶▶ **Now try this!**

How do you interpret the different intonation contours?

    A: I'm SÒRRY#
    A: SÓRRY#
    A: I'm SǑRRY#

[Suggested answer p 216]

Responding to <thanks>

The way we respond to <thanks> is reflected by what we are thanking for, who we are addressing and in what situation:

    [288] A: many THÀNKS#
         B: **RÌGHT#** BÝE# (9.1:165–66)

A female secretary has informed a university administrator of a suitable day for an appointment with her head of department.

    [289] A: well thank you very MÙCH#
        B: **RÍGHT#** . OḰ# (8.2:974–76)

Another female secretary has given a message to a male academic.

    [290] A: ★thanks very MÚCH#★
        B: ★**THÀNK you#.** ★ (8.2:1244–45)

An estate agent has accepted an appointment with a female client later in the week.

<Thanks> predominate in telephone conversations, more

precisely in the closing section just before the leave-taking. The reason is that a number of telephone calls are made for the purpose of getting something done. There was a strong tendency in these calls to use *RÌGHT* when responding to <thanks> or to simply repeat *THÀNKS*, or shift the nucleus from *THÀNK you* to *thank YÒU*.

▶▶▶▶▶ **Now try this!**

How would you respond in polite way to what A says?

    A: THÀNK you# – for the SHÈRRY# – (1.9:547–48)
                              [Suggested answer on p 216]

Re-opening

> The **[re-opener]** reacts to an [initiate] or a [response] and elicits confirmation

Imagine that A comes up with a highly surprising piece of information or that B gives an unexpected <answer> to a <question>. It is highly unlikely that the [response] should consist of a simple <acknowledge>. Aware of their role, conversational partners tend to show surprise, disbelief, or at least interest, rather than indifference.

Re-opening a stating exchange

Consider the following stating exchange from a conversation between a male academic and a female secretary:

    [291] A: ... it was funny going to this SÈM-   [initiate]
              INAR# – on . on . E M Forster's MÀURICE# .
        B: **oh you WÈNT to that#**   [re-open]
        A: YÈS# YÈS# (5.9:1083–87)

If B had responded by *ÒH* alone the effect would have been entirely different. The addition of *you WÈNT to that* does not necessarily indicate that B finds this piece of information so surprising that it needs to be confirmed. It might be added out of pure politeness. The most likely reason according to the context, however, is that A and B had already discussed the seminar in question. Notice that A says **this** SÈMINAR which points to shared knowledge.

The next stating exchange is also interesting. A is telling her husband about a conference at Liverpool University where there had also been a fund-raising drive for the Save the Children Society. HÙGE refers back to *supply* mentioned earlier:

[292] A: I was at Liverpool UNIVÈRSITY# at NUS
   CÒNFERENCE# and there were a − − lot of
   people in the basement handing up . *HÙGE*
  B: *RÉALLY#*
  A: M̀# they probably have quite a few − (4.1:720–25)

B's RÉALLY does not only manage to trigger off confirmation, despite the fact that it comes in the middle of A's turn, but also to interrupt whatever A intended to say. The reason why the conversation does not break down at this point is that A and B share enough background knowledge.

Generally, in a stating exchange, the initiating move is followed by a responding move which terminates the exchange. The exchange pattern is [Initiate] [Response] (cf p 49). If the initiating move triggers off a re-opening move, on the other hand, the pattern becomes [Initiate] [Re-opener] [Response].

Re-opening a questioning exchange

[Re-openers] typically occur in questioning exchanges, following the [response]. They can, for instance, be used to double-check an agreement:

[293] A . . . would twelve o'clock be OKÁY# [initiate]
  B: LÔVELY#   [respond]
  A: **RÍGHT#**   [re-open]
  B: YÈS# (9.1:312–15)

Or they can be used to query a piece of information:

[294] A: tell you who I met YÈSTERDAY# −
  B: WHÈRE#

A: in PICCADÌLLY#
B: WHÒ#
A: Miss LÒCKE#
B: **did you *RÉALLY#***
A: *M̀HM#* – (6.2:903–09)

In the following extract A contemplates the [response] quite a while before he reacts (indicated by – – –):

[295] A: Oscar is GÒING to the States#
B: ((WÈLL))# this is what I HÈARD# just before I came AWÀY# – – –
A: **RÈALLY#**
B: ((YÈS))# (1.2:349–54)

RÈALLY can be interpreted in two ways: either that A finds the information somewhat surprising and wants to have it confirmed, or that he finds the pause embarrassing and feels the need to fill it.

In sum, this is the way we speak if we take the social aspect of conversation seriously, by filling in gaps as it were. In other words, we do not just silently endorse what the other speaker says but we tend to comment on it.

<Re-openers>

all right
OK
really
right
tag Qs

♣♣♣ These items act as [re-openers] only if they are responded to; otherwise they act as [follow-ups] and end of exchange

---

▶▶▶▶ **Now try this!**

Suggest a suitable gap filler.

A: do you think your parents would PÀY for it#
B: no NÒ# . they DÒN'T#
A: _____
B: NÒ# (4.2:1168–73)

[Suggested answer on p 216]

Following up

The [**follow-up**] ratifies the [response]

The study of genuine conversation shows that the [follow-up] is a frequent device in ordinary dialogues and not restricted to the classroom, as has sometimes been claimed. In the classroom, the teacher uses the [follow-up] to indicate, for instance, whether a pupil's <answer> is right or wrong and to show his approval of a good <answer>. Outside the classroom, it is seldom a matter of right or wrong but rather a way of showing an interest and, ultimately, keeping the conversation going.

Following up <questions> and <requests>

[Follow-ups] occur typically in questioning and requesting exchanges:

> [296] **Questioning exchange**
> A: shall we keep those brackets as they ÁRE#
> B: YÈS#
> A: RÌGHT# (9.1:515–17)

RÌGHT serves as a confirmation of a mutual agreement.

> [297] **Requesting exchange**
> A: would you like to take some LÙNCH . *young
>   PÁULINE#*
> B: *M̀# . ((that would))* be very NÌCE PLÉASE# –
> A: ə:m – YÈS# . WÈLL then# we will TÀKE some#
>   – – – (6.2:1038–43)

A seems to hesitate. Does he regret the invitation? Or is he perhaps thinking about where to go? This is not clear. Finally the <accept> is ratified, however.

Imagine that these two exchanges had been terminated by B's [response], which would have been quite possible from a purely 'technical' point of view, ie following the definition of the exchange. From a social point of view, such cut-offs might have a disastrous effect.

[**Follow-ups**]

ah	OK
all right	really
I see	right
oh	tags

♣♣♣ [Follow-ups] are realized by items that are also used as <reacts> and [backchannels]; the tone is typically falling

Summing up, unlike the [re-opener], the [follow-up] does not prompt the other party to respond. It is a kind of final ratifying comment before a new exchange is initiated. Without a [follow-up] the answerer would probably feel less satisfied.

▶▶▶▶▶ **Now try this!**

Suggest a suitable gap filler.

A: what about THÌS# – any GRÁDUATE students here# –
B: you should be meeting those later on – this AFTER-NÒON#
A: _____ (3.3:456–58)

[Suggested answer on p 216]

Accompanying strategies

In addition to the strategies already mentioned, conversation could not do without the following:

* socializing
* hedging
* organizing

Socializing

The main purpose of some conversational strategies is to be 'social', namely:

* backchannelling
* empathizing

Backchannelling was described in Chapters 1 and 2 and will not
be dealt with here. This leaves us with empathizing.

Empathizing

By **empathizing** the speaker intensifies the relationship with the
listener

The fact that <empathizers>, realized by *you know* and *you see*,
often prompt listener feedback, mainly in the form of [backchan-
nels] but also stronger reactions (cf the 'feedback gradient'
pp 81–2), clearly reflects their social function. The current
speaker invites the current listener to take an active part, as it were.

> [298] A: because she felt this was not the moment for votes
>   for WŎMEN# or something of THÀT sort **you**
>   **SÉE#**
>   B: ***how SPLÈNDID#***
> >A: *((it left me quite CÒLD# and)) . . .*   (6.4:
>   723–27)

However, the speaker in [298], does not wait for B to react but
goes on talking, seemingly without paying attention to B's
appreciative comment.

   Similarly, there are many long engaging narrative sections
with a complete lack of audible feedback despite fairly frequent
insertions of especially *you know*. Not even tags, which may also
have a socializing effect, are always followed by listener feedback:

> [299] A: . . . it ÍS a HÒUSEHOLD god of SÓME sort #
>   ÌSN'T it# I should THÍNK# or is it a DÀNCER#
>   I don't KNÒW# it's got an E{NÒRMOUS}
>   BÉLLY# – – –
>   B: M# (1.6:668–74)

Notice that B does not produce M̀ after *ISN'T it* but when the
long pause forces him to say something.

   Maybe the insertion of an <empathizer> is sufficient on its
own from the speaker's point of view. What we cannot conclude
from studying transcripts of conversation, however, is how often

<empathizers> prompt silent feedback, eg in the form of nods and facial gestures.

> **<Empathizers>**
>
> as you know
> if you see what I mean
> you know
> you see
> tags

♣♣♣ <Empathizers> usually occupy a separate tone unit; the tone is most often rising

Hedging

> By **hedging** the speaker modifies what s/he says

Hedging helps the speaker avoid going straight to the point, avoid being blunt, avoid appearing authoritative, and avoid committing him/herself. Hedging is helpful. Maybe the speaker does not know the adequate word or expression, maybe it is convenient not to be straightforward, or maybe s/he thinks the listener is not acquainted with a certain topic or terminology and therefore does not want to place him/her in a face-threatening position.

<Hedges> are especially common in <opines>, ie when the speaker expresses an opinion or attitude to something or somebody:

> [300] A: he was **sort of** INCRÈDIBLY mixed up sort of CHÁP# (1.11:576)

Sort of mitigates *INCRÈDIBLY mixed up.*

> [301] A: **well I think probably** you're RÏGHT# . probably ((. . .)) əm – – that we should pay you on a DÀILY basis# . (9.1:384–85)

This situation is somewhat risky, and the employer had better not commit himself.

Another example is:

[302] a: when ((you probably)) should be − − − glad you've
got involved and are liking it and all .
B: **WÈLL# YÈS# well I mean YǑU know# I've
lived there all this TÍME#** (1.10:426–30)

where the positive effect of YÈS is being moderated by all the
rest.

The prototypical <hedge>, *sort of*, can be paraphrased in a
number of ways. Compare the following:

[303] A: . . . is **sort of** begging for the MǑON# − − ((you
SÉE))# (1.1:743–44)

Sort of is equivalent to 'like';

[304] A: and she was ((**sort of**)) PRÉTTY# (1.3:974)

Sort of is equivalent to 'in a way';

[305] A: no no no it's only about **sort of** − − three months
I think# (1.11:197)

Sort of is equivalent to 'approximately';

[306] A: she doesn't MÌND **sort of**# . FÍXING {THÍNGS#}#
with the CÁR# (1.12:381–83)

Sort of is equivalent to 'it seems';

[307] A: it's just a subject which is − . **sort of** . basically
WELL- KNÓWN# (1.6:849)

Sort of is equivalent to 'more or less'.
It is more difficult to identify what *sort of* is doing in:

[308] A: ((I mean)) I mean she's so LÌTTLE# I mean you
you KNÒW# **sort of** one can IMÀGINE# a **sort
of** middle-aged WÒMAN# with a coat that
seemed . you KNÓW# **sort of**# . just slightly
exaggerated her FÒRM# . you know ((I mean))
she could **sort of** slip things inside PÒCKETS#
(2.13:402–08)

Notice the many instances of *I mean* and *you know* and their
cooccurrence with *sort of*. Maybe they are all used as <fillers>,
with no exact meaning or purpose.

Hedging is achieved in a great number of ways, and it is

sometimes difficult to pinpoint exactly what it is in a speaker's utterance that has the hedging effect. It may be one of the items referred to as interactional signals and discourse markers (pp 58–67), or a modal verb, or a certain type of adverb, or an indirectly put utterance.

<Hedges>	
actually	perhaps
at least	probably
can	quite
generally	rather
hardly	slightly
kind of	sort of
may	tag
ought to	usually

♣♣♣ <Hedges> do not often occupy a separate tone unit; usually, they do not carry a tone

Organizing

Two strategies are involved in organizing the discourse:

* Framing
* Monitoring

Framing

By **framing** the speaker marks a boundary in the discourse

<Frames> can initiate a turn or introduce a new topic (p 85). They can mark a change or a new stage within the speaker's turn, and so on. The following turn, which occurs in a discussion between a university administrator and student representatives, has a <frame> in two places (slots 3 and 4):

[309] A: THǍT'S it# the FÒLKLORE {SOCÍETY library#}#
YÈS# that's that's RÍGHT# that's FÍNE# .
YÈAH# – RÍGHT# . ə:m well N=OW# |jə|
you SǍY in – ÒTHER words# ... (3.3:217–25)

R ĬGHT, marks the end of the discussion so far (the shortage of seats in the English section of the library), and *ə:m well N=OW* introduces a conclusion.

In the next extract, a female studio manager tells a friend about her problems with a former boyfriend. Pay special attention to the two instances of *anyway*, which are obviously doing different things:

> [310] A: ... was trying to drop MÁRTIN# cos he was a
> complete LŎONY# **ANYWAY**# he {RÈALLY
> was} CRÁZY# – =AND# {VÈRY} BŎRING# as
> WÈLL# – . =AND# . **ÁNYWAY**# I – I I must
> have been MÃD to SUGGÈST it# but . Ian needed
> somewhere to STÁY# ... (2.7:670–80)

The first instance has the 'ordinary' grammatical function of conjunct, connecting what is being said with what was said before, while the second instance serves as a <frame>, marking a slight change of direction in the discourse.

Monitoring

> By **monitoring** the speaker can put things right

Sometimes the speaker needs to make a new start or rephrase what s/he was going to say in the middle of a turn, often because the listener shows that s/he cannot follow or is not convinced. In such situations the <monitor> *I mean* comes in handy:

> [311] A: have you . tried at all . so far . **I mean** have you
> ★got round to anything★
> B: ★{NÒ} I HÀVEN'T#★ . **I M=EAN**# . I've done
> NŎTHING# except . you KNŎW# bring up this
> FÀMILY# since I . left SCHÒOL# (3.1:39–46)

Here, both questioner and answerer use *I mean* to make their point clear. Notice *you KNŎW* in B's turn.

I mean tends to collocate with *well*:

> [312] A: I don't BELÌEVE in strange quirky people PÉR-
> SONALLY# I think this is ə: oh **well I mean** .
> NÒ# (2.3:642–43)

and sometimes with *well* in combination with *you know* or *you see*:

[313] A: when I CÓME here you see# . **well I mean**
quarter to SÉVEN **you KNÓW#** – six FÒRTY# (2.5:
165–67)

Another common device is *actually*:

[314] A: things went rather WRÒNG# |ae| **actually** I was
feeling rather GRÒTTY last WÉEK# (9.1:410–11)

Finally, both *sorry* and *pardon me* occurred as <monitors> in
the Corpus.

<Monitors>

actually
I mean
well
well I mean
well you know/you see
well I mean you know/you see

Summing up accompanying strategies

Four accompanying strategies have been described:

* by empathizing the speaker intensifies the relationship with
  the listener;
* by hedging the speaker modifies what s/he says;
* by framing the speaker marks a boundary in the discourse;
* by monitoring the speaker steers what s/he says.

All four strategies contribute to a smooth conversation.

▶▶▶▶ **Now try this!**

What are the boldface items used for in the discourse?

[a] A: you LÌKE it there do you MÓNICA#
B: **well** I love it there in a WÀY## **I mean** I don't
want to stay there FORÉVER# . ÒBVIOUSLY# . or
else it'll be terribly BÀD for me# – **I mean** it's
BÉEN bad ENÓUGH for me as it ÌS I think#
RÉALLY# . in LÒTS of WÁYS# but ə:m – – ə as
{FÀR} as the ARCHAEÓLOGY is concerned# ...
(1.9:783–91)

[b] A: so that is **quite** . **quite a sort of** ÁREA# to DÈAL
with NÓW# − THÈN the DRÀINAGE# W=ELL# − −
Í don't KNÓW# how long that'll take MÓRE# **you
see** the LÀST four years have just# . GÒNE# every
VÁC# you've HEARD# about my poor WRÈTCHED
mother **you know#** HÁVEN'T **you#** (1.9:849−60)
[Suggested answer on p 216]

If you want to know more:

Taking/holding/yielding the turn is described in Beattie (1981),
 Bennett (1981), Brown (1977), Cutler and Pearson (1986),
 Edmondson (1981) Ch.4, Oreström (1983), Stenström (1990a,
 1990b);
backchannelling is described in Schegloff (1982), Stenström (1991),
 Tottie (1989);
exchange procedures are described in Adler (1978), Aijmer (1987),
 Blum–Kulka (1987), Brown et al (1980), Burton (1980), Cheepen
 (1988), Ch.5, Geluykens (1988), Goffman (1976, 1978), Heritage
 (1984), Jefferson (1972), Schegloff (1968), Schegloff et al (1977),
 Stenström (1984, 1988);
accompanying exchange strategies are described in Aijmer (1984),
 Crystal and Davy (1975), Erman (1987), Östman (1981), Svartvik
 (1980);
interactional strategies in general are described in Goffman (1967),
 Gumperz (1982), Schenkein (ed.) (1978).

CHAPTER 4

Conversation

Conversational structure

It sometimes happens that even complete strangers begin a conversation, go on talking for a while and end the conversation without any introductory and terminating procedures whatsoever. This tends to occur when something unexpected happens. Take for instance the occasional brief chat with somebody waiting in the queue at the bus stop when the bus is not on time, or with a fellow-passenger in a train compartment, when there is a sudden stop and nobody tells you why. Brief chats of this kind consist only of 'what is talked about':

| Topic | Message |

The other extreme is a conversation where beginning and end form elaborate patterns and where the message consists of several topics which in their turn are made up of a number of subtopics:

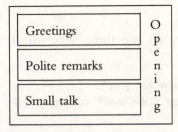

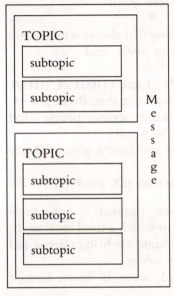

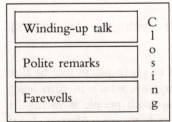

Two 'ordinary' conversations

The overall pattern of face-to-face conversation varies largely with the situation and depends on such factors as where the conversation takes place, who is talking to whom and what the talk is about. The overall pattern of telephone calls is more fixed. Telephone calls always contain an **opening**, and a **closing**, for instance, with certain set actions involved.

Talking face-to-face

Four academics, one female (speaker A) and three male, meet after work for a drink and a chat:

> [315] a: Geoffrey Ramsden *how are you*
> A: *oh HELLO# I've been LONGING* to see you#
> *how ARE you#*
> B: *it's AGES since* I've seen you#
> a: *((several sylls))*
> A: *YES# . I've been asking ((I)) always sending you
> MESSAGES# – *but* you never send
> B: *OH#*
> A: any messages BACK# *so I got TIRED of THIS#
> B: *do you REALLY# I don't get them# (laughs–)*
> A: YES#* – I always keep seeing people and
> S=AYING# . how's GEOFFREY#
> a: hello he*llo Dai* come and have a glass of sherry
> man
> A: *HELLO#* – – how nice to SEE you# (1.9:1–20)

The recording begins when the host (speaker a) introduces himself to A. Some small talk follows in which a third speaker, B, takes part. When speaker C turns up, drinks are being offered and the 'warming-up' talk continues for a while.

The first real topic is introduced, when B directs himself to A:

> [316a] B: are you in TOUCH with the St {BEE'S}
> CROWD# . (1.9:81)

A remarks that there is really no need to go to places like St Bee since everybody comes to London anyway, which in turn leads on to 'the trouble of having to put up with people who find it convenient to come to London', and so on. After a brief interchange about A's sabbatical term there is a sudden switch to an entirely different topic.

Prompters like the following set people going:

> [316b] a: well what's what's going on in Surroford give us
> the dirt . come on (1.9:272)

And the following leads on to a chat about pubs:

[316c] C: come ÓN# what's the what's the dirt in Rufford
ITSÉLF# let's have the RÚFFORD DÌRT# –
YÈS# (1.9:330–33)

It goes on until somebody mentions a pub called the
Scarborough, which reminds C of an appointment:

[316d] C: ((that)) REMÌNDS me# I'm GÒING# (1.9:
512–13)

He leaves and that is the end of that part of the conversation:

[316e] C: ə (coughs –) THÀNKS# ((2 sylls))
a: pardon
C: THÀNK you# – *for the SH*ÈRRY#* –
a: *(laughs –)* a great pleasure Dai (1.9:545–49)

The conversation as a whole is very informal, and what is talked
about is restricted to personal things rather than facts. There is a
great deal of overlapping speech, often caused by the offering of
drinks. There is structure, however. It can be described as
follows: <greetings> – phatic talk – chat – phatic talk – farewell
<greetings>.

Talking on the telephone

The following brief telephone call is an excellent example of the
'routine' structure of telephone conversation:

[317] A: HELLÓ#
B: Mr HÙRD# . it's Professor CLÁRK's
secretary# *from Paramilitary* CÒL-
LEGE#–   } Opening
A: *oh YÉS#*

B: Professor Clark asked if you were .
going to collect some SCRÌPTS {TO-
NÌGHT#}# *SÒUND* scripts# .   } Message
A: *YÈS#* ((MHM))#

B: if you'd collect them from Mr GÒR-
DON# *who will be going to* |ði:|
PLÀ meeting#   } Message
A: *Mr GÓRDON#* YÈS# ((=M#))

B: RÍGHT#
A: Y=ES# *thanks* very MÚCH#
B: *(– giggles)* OḰ# . ə B=YE# ⎤ Closing
A: B=YE# ⎦
(9.1:713–32)

There is an opening which includes answering the telephone signal and identifying answerer and caller, a message section containing a <request> followed by acceptance, and a closing which involves reconfirming the agreement just made, thanking and bidding farewell.

In the opening, it is the answerer who picks up the phone and answers the call and the caller who makes sure who the answerer is and identifies himself before coming to the reason for the call. In the message section, it is the caller who provides the first topic, (in this case at least) the reason for the call. The closing is initiated by the caller. Finally it is the answerer who bids farewell.

Clearly, there is variation. Some calls are even shorter and have very brief opening, message and closing sections, while others may require quite intricate openings, with message sections of almost indefinite length, and closings interrupted and temporarily held up by new upcoming talk.

Topical framework

The message of a conversation, what the conversation is about, is developed within a topical framework. A brief telephone call, for instance, often has a single message, ie one topic. Half an hour's face-to-face conversation, on the other hand, can contain anything from a main topic divided into subtopics to a series of more or less related topics.

The message

Let's go back to the four academics talking in [316] and look at the message in more detail [316f].

The first topic, 'the St Bee's Crowd', changes into 'uninvited friends turning up in London'. There is a sudden switch to 'B's sabbatical' (*have you got a* – LÉAVE NÓW) and a new sudden switch to 'A's hurt finger' (*what's happened to your finger*) which changes into 'C's work on the railways' (where fingers get caught in doors), and so on.

All in all, as many as eight more or less closely related topics are dealt with in about a quarter of an hour's time. Only once is there a clear indication that there is nothing more to say about a topic, taking the form of a long pause. The topical framework has the following shape (text 1.9):

[316f]

> B: are you in TÒUCH with the St BÉE'S CRÓWD

> A: this is the very əm this'll obviously is the BÀD thing about living in LÓNDON

> B: have you got a LÈAVE NÓW – SABBÀTICAL

> a: *what's happ*ened to your finger

– – –

> C: *when I* worked on the RÁILWAYS

> a: well what's going on in Surroford give us the dirt

> a: *well as a matter of fact – * last week I didn't tell you this

> C: come ÓN what's the what's the dirt in Rufford ITS⌄ELF

For strategies used to introduce a new topic, see pp 85–7, 151–2.

Conversational structure and the discourse hierarchy

A conversation is a piece of discourse containing one or more topics. According to the definition of a transaction (p 30), each topic corresponds to a transaction in the discourse hierarchy, the immediately lower level of which is the exchange. The message section of the telephone call, example [317], is consequently equivalent to one transaction consisting of one requesting exchange. In the face-to-face conversation, exemplified in [316a–316e] and repeated in [316f], the message section is much more complex. There are eight topics, corresponding to eight transactions, all of them consisting of more than one exchange.

Conversational strategies

Conversational strategies differ not only depending on the actual situation, eg in terms of topic, degree of formality and medium, but also depending on how far the conversation has proceeded. This section concentrates on openings and closings. What the speakers talk about will be dealt with separately (pp 150–62).

How to open a conversation

Most conversations begin with an opening before the message is introduced. Some face-to-face conversations lack an opening altogether. Openings are different; there are conventional, formal, speaker-specific, situation-specific openings, and so on.

Face-to-face openings

Face-to-face openings will be described according to the following classification:

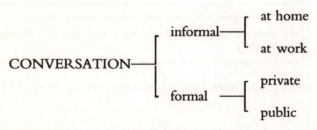

An informal conversation at home
A female studio manager, C, has been invited for supper to a married couple, a and b. All three are in their early 20's, and the atmosphere is very relaxed:

[318] a: *hello*
C: *HELLÓ#* . sorry I'm LÁTE#
a: *(. laughs) that's alright* are you –
b: *(– laughs murmur)*
C: YÈS# . I said half past SÉVEN#
a: oh I expected you between about . – half past and
quarter to
C: hello LÍZ# . sorry I'm LÁTE# (– laughs)
b: oh I like your hair
C: M̀#
a: yes Ann you've had it curled
C: |jìz|# (. laughs)
a: yes that's nice – I say that's nice (2.7:1–17)

The most characteristic features are the informal <greetings> (*hello*
– HELLÓ), the laughters and the spontaneous compliment (*oh I like
your hair*) instead of the usual inquiries about health. This is all
part of the phatic talk which continues while C is offered a drink,
and it goes on for quite a while.

An informal conversation at work
Two male academics, A and B, meet for a talk in A's office. A is
busy making coffee when B arrives, which explains the disturbing
noise that causes the many inaudible syllables. This conversation
also begins with a <greeting>, but it is not responded to:

[319] A: Richard HALLÒ# . I've just *|s|* set out
B: *thank YÒU#*
>A: *((syll SÝLL#* make some))
B: *THÀNKS#*
>A: I've just boiled some WÀTER# *for having
CÒFFEE#* cos I haven't HÀD
B: *((3 to 4 sylls))*
A: time for TÉA# *would* you LÍKE some#
B: *YÈS#* YÈS#
A: THÀNKS# for your INVITÁTION# you |həu|
throwing a *PÀRTY#*
B: *YÈS#* (1.4:1–13)

The most striking feature is perhaps not just the amount of simultaneous speech but the fact that A and B are able to communicate
despite it. It is difficult to decide who to admire most, A who does
not lose patience but manages to go on talking, or B who seems to be
able to anticipate whatever A is going to say.

A formal conversation at work

A 30-year-old male academic, speaker B, who is a newcomer in the department, meets three of his new colleagues, all male and around 50, to discuss the curriculum and inform them about his previous experience as a teacher:

[320] A: good MÒRNING# .
      B: good MÒRN*ING#*
      A: *my* name's WÉLLA# .
      B: |=əhə|#
      A: ə: it may be that {YÒU {KNÒW#}} if only by
         SÌGHT# some of the people {HÉRE} in the
         DEPÁRTMENT# – Doctor *PÉREGRINE# – Derek
         HÓPITZ# – – Steve LÉAGRE#*
      B: *ə: – YÉS# ((2 to 3 sylls)) by SÌGHT# YÈS#*
      ? *YÈS# YÈS#* YÈS# we HÀVE met#
    >A: Professor DRÁKE#
      B: YÈS# .
      A: ə: come and sit HĚRE will you# ə:m . Dizzy
         GRŎOMLITE# is ə: ə: is ((on)) *just about to
         RETÙRN#*
      a: *just coming back* – –
      C: *SÒRRY#*
      A: *here* he ÌS# .
      C: YÉAH# ((it's)) ÀLL right# – – – HELLÒ# .
      B: HELLÒ# – – – (3.6:1–28)

After the exchange of <greetings>, A goes on to introduce himself and the other members of staff, using their academic titles. This is all rather formal. C is less formal than A, however, judging by his *HELLÒ*. Notice that the simultaneous speech occurs only when A introduces the members of staff to B. It does not seem to block the communication.

A public conversation

This is the beginning of a radio conversation, and as such tailor-made for the listeners. Those taking part in the conversation represent three generations: a male radio producer, A, his old father, B, who is a retired lawyer, and his 24-year old daughter (C) (who does not enter the conversation at once):

[321] A: W=ELL# I've brought us – . TOG{ÉTHER}# ÌN
         the studio# cos I think there ÀRE# . really rather
         UN{ÌQUE}# ÈLEMENTS# ÌN our relationship#

– ə: one of the things ÌS# {I THÌNK#}# |ðiː| .
gap between our ÂGES# ə: GR=AMPY# . you were
. forty-TWÒ# when Ì was BÓRN# –
B: YÉS# (6.4:1–11)

Due to the aim of the conversation, A gives a rough presentation of the participants to begin with and then turns to his father for the first comment. The most striking feature in this presentation is perhaps the way A emphasizes what he says by placing nuclear stress on unexpected words, eg adjacent words (TOGÈTHER ÎN, UNÌQUE ÈLEMENTS ÎN). Notice also that the pauses are used for emphasis rather than hesitation I've brought us – . TOGÈTHER, there ÂRE . really, you were . forty-TWÒ). More about this conversation follows on pp 181–4.

Telephone openings

The way telephone openings are realized is very much tied to who answers and in what capacity. The following categories of call will be considered:

★ calls answered by a telephonist
★ calls answered by a secretary
★ calls answered by a person in charge
★ calls answered by an individual

A diagram reveals the complexity:

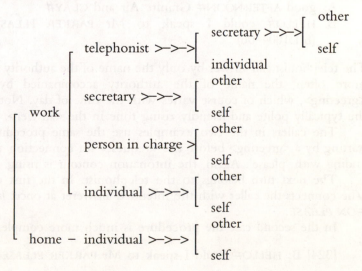

Home calls are the least complicated ones. If there is a [response], you either get in touch with the person you want to talk to at once (unless there is an answering machine) or, if the person is at home, with the intermediary of a member of the family. When you call somebody at work and you do not have the intended person's direct number you will either have to go via a telephonist who connects you with the person in question, or with a secretary who then connects you with the person you want to talk to, or you can call the secretary directly and ask to be connected.

A call that reaches the end of the chain can be official or private in nature.

Calls answered by a telephonist
Switchboard-operated openings are the most impersonal ones for obvious reasons. They are also the ones that follow the most rigidly conventional pattern. The telephone signal is typically answered in one of the following ways, and the answer is followed by the caller's request for connection:

[322] **name of authority**
A: VÁUXHALL School# – –
B: HELLÓ# may I speak to Jo JÚDD please# (7.2:1330–32)

[323] **<greeting> + name of authority**
A: good AFTERNÓON# Granite Air and CLÁY#
B: HÈLLO# could I speak to Mr PÀRKER PLÉASE# (8.1:1004–06)

The telephonist can answer by only the name of the authority or, more often, the name of the authority accompanied by a <greeting>, which of course varies with the time of day. Notice the typically polite and friendly rising tone in the <answer>.

The callers in the two examples use the same procedure, starting by a <greeting> before the <request> for connection and ending with 'please'. Again, the intonation contour is rising.

The next turn belongs to the telephonist. In the first call s/he connects the caller with the intended answerer at once: *hold* =ON PLÈASE.

In the second case the procedure is much more complex:

[324] B: HÈLLO# could I speak to Mr PÀRKER PLÉASE#

A: **who's** CÁLLING#
B: it's Doctor ÈDGTON# –
A: əm . **can you tell me what it's in** CONNÉCTION **with#** *Doc*tor ÈDGTON# –
B: *Y=ES# – well he ə:m . ə ə ə . phoned me earlier this MÓRNING# about ə:m some FLÀTS# in {Barn HÌLL#}# . əm and asked me to ring BÀCK# in FÀCT#
A: ÒH# right ÓH# hold ÓN#
B: thank Y=OU# – – – (8.1:1006–19)

Not only does the telephonist want to know who is calling but also the reason for calling before she connects the call. This obviously puts the caller (Dr Edgton) somewhat off balance judging by the filled pauses at the beginning of her turn.

Compare the next opening. A female university lecturer calls an estate agency and puts forward a <request> (reason for calling) at once, apparently not knowing who to ask for:

[325] A: LÉWISHAM#
B: good MÓRNING# I wonder if you could put me on your MÂILING list please# {for PRÔPERTIES#}# (8.2:1–3)

This beginning demands more action on the part of the telephonist, who continues:

[326] A: ə:m . what were you LÓOKING for#
B: ə:m . ((a)) FLÁT# or a small HÓUSE# . up to about eleven and a half THÔUSAND# (8.2:4–8)

As soon as she knows what the caller wants she can connect the call to the person in charge.

Calls answered by a secretary
Secretaries tend to answer calls in one of the ways exemplified below. The caller is then expected to reveal her/his reason for calling, which may be to make an enquiry or ask for somebody else, as in [327], or simply have a friendly chat with the secretary, as in [328]:

[327] A: Professor MÂINE's office# .
B: ÓH# is Mrs DÁVY there please# . (9.1:698–700)

[328] A: Regimental SUBADÁR'S secretary#
　　　B: how're you FÈELING# . (7.2:1276–77)

The caller in [327] seems to have expected Mrs Davy to pick up
the receiver, judging by the surprised ÓH at the beginning of the
turn. [328] is not an entirely private call despite the familiar tone.
It turns out that the caller wants some information in the end.

　　A simple *hello* causes problems. It always forces the caller to
make sure who s/he is talking to before proceeding:

[329a] A: HELLǑ#
　　　　B: HELL=O# ə:m ə:m is that Babcock WÒRTH'S
　　　　　　ə: SÉCRETARY# (9.1:248–50)

The caller is at a loss and needs to be reassured before he goes on:

[329b] A: it íS#
　　　　B: ə:m it's Bill GRǍVY# – ə: from MÁRTIN# –
　　　　　　(9.1:251–54)

Hello <answers> are rare in public contexts for obvious reasons.
Answering the phone at home is different; then a simple *hello* is
more likely and generally also more acceptable.

Calls answered by a person in charge
Some business establishments have no switchboard, and calls are
answered directly by a member of staff, eg a salesman, as in the
following example. Such calls tend to be particularly polite:

[330] A: SÉWING-machine centre# good AFTERNǑON# .
　　　B: good AFTERNÒON# – ə:m do you stock
　　　　　NÈCCHI MACHÍNES# – (8.1:444–47)

The caller goes straight to the point as in the previous example,
but in this case that is no problem since the person in charge
answers at once, and the conversation can go on, beginning with
an inviting YÉS.

Calls answered by an individual
A person answering his own telephone at work or at home can
choose one of the following ways. Whichever way s/he chooses
may have consequences for the next few turns. What is important
is to know who is at the other end:

[331] **the answerer says** *hello*
　　　A: *HELLÓ#*

B: *hello* Pelham DÓLMETCHSON speaking# .
A: |h| HELLÓ# it's MÁY# –
B: ÒH# (7.3:1306–10)

The answerer identifies herself in turn three.

[332] the answerer identifies her/himself
A: Wintermere SPÉAKING# –
B: HELLÓ#
A: HĚLLO#
B: CHÀRLIE#
A: YĚS#
B: ((actually)) it's
A: HELLÒ Karen# (7.2:939–45)

The speakers are apparently on first-name terms only, so B is not much helped by hearing A's second name. It is not until turn seven that A and B have established their mutual identities.

[333] the answerer gives her/his office number
A: ((EXTÈNSION)) five |əu| TWÓ# .
B: (. giggles) HELLÓ# .
A: HÌ# .
B: how are YÒU# (7.2:677–81)

These speakers can settle down to business at once. They obviously recognize each other's voices.

[334] the answerer gives her/his home number
A: seven one seven NÍNE# .
B: JĚAN# .
A: oh HULLÓ Annie# (7.2:176–78)

The same refers to these two speakers.

[335] the answerer gives her/his office/home number
+ name
A: three three . SHĚILA Johnstone#
B: can I speak to JÌM Johnstone please# (9.1:1132–33)

In this case, finally, there is no reason for confusion.

It is in the nature of things that the answerer speaks first and also that the caller provides the first topic. The <answer> is typically pronounced with a rising tone signalling expectation. A simple *hello* can obviously cause problems and is definitely out of place in official contexts, where it is of crucial importance for the caller to know who s/he is talking to before going on to business. And in a private context it would hardly be possible to communicate at all without mutual identification or recognition.

Summing up face-to-face and telephone openings

Face-to-face and telephone openings have the following features in common:

- the parties greet each other
- phatic talk usually precedes the topic

They are different in the following respects:

- telephone but not face-to-face openings require speaker identification
- in a telephone conversation it is the caller who brings up the first topic; in face-to-face conversation there is no such rule

▶▶▶▶▶ **Now try this!**

Where would you place these telephone openings in the diagram presented on page 143?

[a]   a: hello Ann it's Joan
      B: HELLÒ {JÒAN#}#
      a: (sings Happy Birthday)
      B: (sings dialect to you) THÀNK you# (– laughs) I
          DÌD have {a nice BÍRTHDAY#}#
      a: you did (7.1:1370–71)

[b]   A: REGIMÈNTAL SUBADÁR'S secretary# .
      B: how're you FÉELING# .
      A: ÒH HELLÓ# – not too BÁD# – . (7.2:1276–80)

[c]   A: HELLÓ# nine one double eight five |/əu|#
      B: HELL=O# (7.3:921–23)

[d]   A: just a MÒMENT please# (– – –)
      C: HELLÓ# –
      B: Miss BÁRKER#
      C: YÉS# (8.2:931–35)

[Answer on p 217]

How to create an atmosphere

Before a topic is introduced in a conversation, there is generally a warming-up period of varying length, where the parties engage in so-called **phatic talk**. [336] is a particularly good example. Two female students have met. They have just exchanged <greetings> and this is how the conversation begins:

[336a] A: – – – you got a CŎLD#
 B: – NŎ# . just a bit SNĬFFY# cos I'm – I ÀM
 CŎLD# and I'll be all right once I've warmed
 ÙP# – do I LŎOK as though I've got a CŎLD#
 A: no I thought you SŎUNDED as if you were#
 (1.3:6–12)

Then, B starts complaining about her busy day:

[336b] B: .. I had about five thousand BŎOKS# – to take
 back to Senate HŎUSE YÉSTERDAY# – and I got
 all the way through the CŎLLEGE# to where the
 CÀR was# . . . and realized I'd left my .
 CÒAT# in my LŎCKER#. . . (1.3:27–31)

This leads over to the weather:

[336c] A: it's gone very CŎLD# HÀSN'T it#
 B: M̂# – – – it's FRÊEZING# (1.3:42–45)

And a brief chat about knitting and sewing leads on to the first real topic, which is properly introduced by a <metacomment> and a <preface>:

[336d] B: – – something I want to go BÁCK to# – I
 acquired an absolutely magnificent SÈWING-
 MACHINE# by foul MÈANS# did I TÈLL you
 about THÁT# (1.3:95–98)

Phatic talk is also used to wind up a conversation, as in the extract below. Two male academics have been discussing the job situation in the department, when A realizes that it is getting late:

[337] A: – – – what time is your – BŎAT train# or
whatever it

B: *PLÁNE#* .

A: PLÁNE is it#

B: YĔAH# YĔAH#

A: ÂH#

B: ((because)) . YĔS# – – I've got to be at London
Airport at FŎURISH#

A: ŎH#

B: going over to DĬLLONS# to buy some BŎOKS#
– .

A: ə:m – – . ((I'll)) just put this back in the .
SŬRVEY#

B: *((I will))#*

A: ŎH# THÁNK you very MÚCH# . if you'd be so
KÍND# very KÍND of you# . I'm going out
SHŎPPING# .

B: WĔLL then# THĂNKS for the CÓFFEE#

A: great PLÉASURE# glad to SĔE you# BYĔ#

B: BYĔ# (3.2:717–41)

Phatic talk usually has the following ingredients:

- questions about health
- comments on the weather
- comments on personal matters
- polite phrases

How to deal with topics

The **topic** is what the speakers talk about

The message section of a conversation consists of the topic(s)
dealt with. Some conversations contain only one topic, but since
one topic has a tendency to generate another (especially in purely
social interaction), most conversations contain more than one. A
topic tends to split into **subtopics** dealing with particular aspects
of the main topic.

The following topical strategies are involved:

* introducing and terminating
* changing, shifting and drifting
* digressing and resuming

Introducing and terminating

Introducing a topic

> **Introducing** involves bringing up a first topic at the beginning or a new topic in the course of the conversation

The first topic is most likely to be introduced by means of some linguistic strategy which helps the speaker to get started and prepares the listener for the speaker's next action. Take, for instance, the following exchange from the informal conversation between the two female academics introduced in [336]. After a couple of minutes' phatic talk A says:

> [338] A: – – **something I ((want)) to go BÁCK to#** – I acquired an absolutely magnificent SÉWING-MACHINE# by foul MÈANS# **did I TÈLL you about THÁT#** B: NÒ# (1.3:95–99)

First, *something I ((want)) to go BÁCK to* prepares B, the listener, for A's next action. Second, *did I TÈLL you about THÁT*, makes certain that B has not already heard the story and, what is more, it saves A from making a fool of herself by telling the same story twice (cf 'prefacing' pp 86–7).

Certain linguistic items, like *right*, *well* and *now*, can either introduce a topic on their own or precede some other introductory strategy, as in [339], where a lecturer is just starting to talk while drawing a picture on the board:

> [339] A: **RÍGHT#** . **so what I'm going to {DÈMON-STRATE} HÉRE#** . is . |ði:| . DÍFFERENCE# BETWÈEN# a TRÁNSVERSE wave# . and a longitudinal WÁVE# . (10.7:869–73)

In spontaneous conversations, with speakers who know each other well and share a great deal of common ground, the first

topic may be embarked upon straightaway. This is where
<questions> come in very handy:

[340] A: how did you get on at your ÌNTERVIEW# .
(1.3:25)

Less often a new topic is launched by a <statement>:

[341] A: **it went off very SMÒOTHLY#** *((at))*
    B: *AHÀ#*
    >A: **that meeting** of the executive COMMÌTTEE#
    (1.2:1–3)

A case like [341] presupposes that A takes for granted that B
knows that there was going to be a meeting. Otherwise A would
first have introduced the topic. Notice the marked word-order,
however, which partly makes up for the lack of an introductory
marker. In order to highlight the **topical word**, A moves it from
its ordinary initial position and replaces it in its proper place by a
pronoun, '**it** went off . . . **that meeting**'.

Similar strategies are used to introduce new topics as the
conversation continues, but as will become obvious, there is a
strong tendency in everyday conversation just to drift (pp 157–8)
from one topic to the next.

Terminating a topic

> **Terminating** involves closing the old topic before introducing a
> new one or before closing the entire conversation

Linguistic termination markers are rare. This is one of the few:

[342] A: that's all he SÁYS# . SHÒULD be ENÓUGH#
    B: **well that's** ÌT# *((let's pass))*
    A: *this P=OLLY#* – you know that G=IRL# . . .
    (1.4:883–88)

But even if all terminations are not linguistically marked,
they are still not entirely unmarked. Silent pauses, for instance,
may serve as termination markers, as in [343], confirmed as it
were by M̂:

343] A: . . . or is it a DÀNCER# I don't KNÒW# it's got
    an E{NÒRMOUS} BÈLLY# – – –
    B: M̂# – – –

A: how do you get ÒN with {THÒRPE#}#
(1.6:671–75)

Laughter is another non-lexical termination marker, as in the following extract from a pre-Christmas dinner conversation:

[344] A: I'll tell you WHÁT# we'll go ÉARLY# –(5 seconds untranscribable speech and laughter)
      B: WÈLL# do you do yours still hang up a STÒCKING# . (4.3:978–82)

In other cases the current topic comes gradually to an end, and there is no need for a marker to indicate the termination. In [345] it is pretty obvious that both A and B realize that there is nothing more to say:

[345] A: well Amy |wə:| Amy kept sort of . hugging her little white SHÀWL round her# and saying I wish I hadn't knitted HÒLES into this#
      B: (–*–* laughs)
      A: *(laughs –)* and quite WHŶ she was feeling# CÒLD# I ((don't)) cos Í ((would have)) thought it was# {|tέsprətli|} HÒT# you KNÒW# I mean I not that I MÌNDED# – the WÁRMTH TO{DÁY#}# at ÀLL#
      B: m
      A: əm – –
      B: m
      A: ÀNYWAY# – we must – . consider SÉRIOUSLY# – the PRÒM programme# . (2.11:120–37)

A pretext for leaving is a most forceful termination marker in that it terminates not just the current topic but the entire conversation:

[346] A: *...* I must watch the TÌME Reynard#
      B: *((QU=ITE))# =M#*
      >B: ((or I may miss the BÀNK))# (1.1:1201–04)

The shortest version of termination markers occurs, in particular, in telephone conversation:

[347] A: ... and all the RÈST of it# but |em| . ÀNYWAY# . I'll have to put it FÒRWARD to them#
      B: OK̀# well thanks for RÌNGING# . (8.1:433–37)

Termination markers are also realized by *alright* and especially *right*.

Termination markers

all right
OK
right
that's it
there we are

♣♣♣ Items used as terminating markers are partly the same as those used as introductory markers and change and shift markers

Changing, shifting and drifting

Changing the topic

Changing involves abandoning the current topic in favour of a new, unrelated, topic

---

A new topic can be introduced in the course of the on-going conversation after the previous topic has been properly terminated by an explicit lexical marker:

> [348] A: do we now write a NÒTE#
> B: WÈLL# NÒ# I {think ((NÒ#}# do)) you SÉE# that's what I've DÓNE#
> A: ⋆ÒH#⋆
> B: ⋆that's⋆ all he SÀYS# . SHÒULD be ENÓUGH#
> A: **well# that's ÌT#** ⋆((let's pass))⋆
> B: ⋆((**this P=OLLY#**⋆ . you know **that G=IRL#** whom I've |m| I I |m m| presented . ((a)) rather ABSÙRD report in a way ((that)) genuinely represented what I FÈLT# I ((said)) **she** might FAIL# . . . do you KNÒW her# (1.4:877–97)

A terminates the old topic by (*well# that's ÌT*) and tries to go on to something new (*let's pass*), when B interrupts and brings up a new topic. The lack of introductory marker is compensated for by a strategic manipulation of the <question> form; the topical element *this P=OLLY* is moved to front position for greater emphasis (cf 'fronting' pp 98–9).

In [349], A terminates the old topic (RÌGHT) and goes on to the next in the same turn (WÈLL *now switching to*):

[349] A: ə:m . **RÌGHT# WÈLL now#** switching to . ə: **your return to this** CÒUNTRY# ... (3.2: 102–03)

In less casual situations, such as discussions and meetings, introductory markers are usually realized by a fairly limited set of interrogative and imperative expressions:

[350] A: ə:m – let me just ÀSK# INÍTIALLY THÌS# (2.6:442–43)

[351] A: can I ÀSK you as WÓMAN vice-president# (3.3:908)

[352] A: can I just tell a story HÉRE# (6.4:345)

Despite their form, such expressions do not trigger a [response], nor are they meant to be responded to; they are only used as a convenient and polite means of taking the floor.

In informal conversations between intimate speakers new topics tend to be brought up at once, as in the following extract from the husband-wife conversation:

[353] B: I didn't hear the news before I came ÓUT# . I'd LÈFT# . well BEFÒRE that# .

A: **I wonder ((when))** |benə| **. when . Bernadette will be** ARRÌVING# .

B: I don't KNÒW# but she's very welcome to come up for a MÉAL# – – – (4.1:881–86)

Informal markers	Formal markers
what else	can I ask you
did I tell you	let me tell you
do you know	let me ask you
I wonder	

Shifting the topic

> **Shifting** involves moving from one topic to a related topic or from
> one aspect of the current topic to another

Like topic changes, topic shifts may be initiated by a marker. The
difference is that it now marks the **transition** between an old and
a new topic instead of introducing an entirely new topic:

> [354] A: ... now this is a a GÒRGEOUS# lazy way
>   ÒUT# you SÉE# he's TÁKEN ÌN by THÍS# dear
>   SÓUL# (– laughs) a*bid*ing faith in
>   B: *m*
>   *(– coughs)*
> >A: *English LÌT*ERATURE# YÒU KNÓW#
>   B: – I . REMÈMBER# **it isn't quite the same**
>   **THÌNG#** but a a PÈRSON . when I was at
>   SCHÒOL# ... (1.6:287–98)

The old and the new topic are clearly related; *quite the same
THÌNG* refers back to what A was talking about and which is
summed up in *this is a a GÒRGEOUS lazy way ÒUT.*

When linguistic markers are entirely missing, transitions tend
to be marked by pauses and/or laughter. The new aspect, or
subtopic, may then be initiated by a <statement>:

> [355] A: ... I'm sure he went for a SMÓKE# **(– – laughs) –**
>   **–**
>   B: **I did know one Indian who . IRÒNICALLY# –**
>   **learnt to CHÁINSMOKE# in this CÒUNTRY#**
>   ... (1.6:608–12)

or, more often, a <question>:

> [356] A: ... he could break it in HÓLIDAYS# – – but as
>   soon as the TÈRM began AGÁIN# – . the strain
>   was too MÙCH# ((for him to)) . couldn't *((go
>   and do)) without them any LÒNGER#*
>   B: *(– – . laughs)* **what part of India were YÒU**
>   **in#** (1.6:642–46)

A and B have been talking about this Indian colleague for a

while, and since A has spent some time in India it is only natural that the conversation should lead over to his stay there more or less automatically.

Shift markers

actually
by the way
in (actual) fact
incidentally
now
talking about
that reminds me
well
what about

♣♣♣ Introductory markers and shift markers are partly realized by the same items

Drifting from the topic

Drifting involves moving almost imperceptibly from one topic to another

---

Drifting is shifting in an inconspicuous way. Topic drifts are linguistically unmarked, but there is usually some associative link between the old and the new topic. The following extract is a good illustration. The speakers are talking about various places to go for a holiday. A mentions Dorset, and as soon as she does, speaker b is reminded of a mutual friend whose parents own a house in the area. Suddenly the conversation is all about the friend's parents:

[357] A: I love DÓRSET though# it's so BÉAUTIFUL# – – .
b: Ian's ties with it are about to be broken
A: ÁRE *they#*
b: *cos* **his parents are selling their house** or trying to .
A: ÓH# that's SÁD# (2.7:1216–22)

Nothing marks the transition, neither lexis nor prosody. Such topic drifts are particularly common when the main aim of the conversation is being social.

Digressing and resuming

Digressing from the topic

Digressing involves moving away temporarily from the current topic

---

Some digressions are **spontaneous**, others are **deliberate**. Some digressions are clearly related to the current topic, others seem to be completely unrelated. [358] below is from a radio discussion with an audience present in the studio. The current topic is the question of whether it is possible for a family of five to live on unemployment pay. At this point in the discussion it is time for a pun:

> [358] A: ... **INCIDÉNTALLY#** I did ÒNCE# **know a**
> **man who lived on GRÀSS#** –
> B: YÈS# so did Ì#
> aud: (– – laughter)
> B: I understand he's DÈAD {NÒW#}#
> C: YÈS# – can I ... (5.4:707–15)

And the discussion goes back to normal. As you will have noticed, the digression is closely related to the current topic, which is already hinted at by *INCIDÉNTALLY*.

Other digressions have no connection, or at least no obvious connection, with the current topic. In the following telephone conversation, for instance, A and B have been talking about domestic matters when B suddenly remembers that she has promised to deliver a message:

> [359] A: ... I'll keep an ÉYE open for it# –
> B: ÓK# – =AND# **by the WÀY#** I forgot to TÈLL
> **you#** last NÌGHT# that ə:m – – Bill PÒTTER-
> TON# wants us to go round on Sunday |ə:|
> AFTERNÒON# . (7.2:85–92)

Like the digression in [358], this digression is linguistically marked, but notice that although both *by the way* and *incidentally* are used when the speaker wants to add something that s/he has just come to think of, there is a slight difference between the two in that *incidentally* but not *by the way* tends to add information that is related to the current topic.

Other digressions are linguistically unmarked but prosodically marked. Take the following, for instance, which comes in the middle of a discussion about B's background:

> [360] A: əm it's in LÌNCOLNSHIRE# –
> B: =UHUH# –
> A: {PÀRT of} KÉSTEVEN# – – – **Thorpe's AWÁY is**
> **he#** (1.6:183–86)

This digression may not be entirely spontaneous. The long pause after *KÉSTEVEN* seems to reflect that there is a momentary gap to be filled. The digression does not come straight out of the blue, however; the conversation takes place in a university department, and Thorpe happens to be the much discussed head of this department. Laughs and giggles terminate the digression and mark the resumption of the old topic.

Some digressions are clearly deliberate, made for the purpose of clarifying and getting clarification and additional information:

> [361] A: . . .HÈ# wasn't a very GÒOD lecturer# in
> FÀCT# ((he)) . wrote very very CL=EAR#
> L=UCID and ((untranscribable murmur))
> B: **where did you RÈAD#**
> A: **CÀMBRIDGE#**
> B: M̌# – –
> A: it was ə: – WÈLL# the CÒURSE# was well
> thought ÒUT# . there was nothing wrong with it
> at ÀLL# it was just his MÀNNER# . (1.6:816–26)

The fact that A studied at Cambridge has no direct importance for the understanding but adds to the information value of what A says.

Digression markers

actually
as a matter of fact
by the way
I mean
incidentally

Resuming the topic

> **Resuming the topic** involves ending the digression and going back
> to the old topic

The speaker who broke out of the current topic also usually takes
the initiative to go back:

    [362] A: ⋆ . . . we didn't wrap ÙP for you#⋆
            B: ⋆oh INCIDÉNTALLY ə:# . ə: |j j| you know⋆
               about MÀLCOLM# . ə: putting his dislocating his
               SHÒULDER# . . . .
            B: **no I wouldn't like to TÒUCH it# I'd put
               DÍRTY FÍNGER-MARKS on it** (laughs – –)
               (4.4:179–233)

B initiated the digression (*oh INCIDÉNTALLY*) and it is also B
who resumes the old topic, 'unwrapping presents'. In [363], on
the other hand, the digression leads over to a topic shift. A and B
were talking about B's background, when B suddenly asks about
the creature sitting on Thorpe's desk:

    [363] A: . . . that was – – . oh well how long would THÀT
               be# – two YÉARS# – – four and half year
               ÌNTERVAL#
            B: M̀ – – – ((what's)) that thing that THÒRPE'S
               got# sitting on his DÈSK# there# . . . it's got an
               E{NÒRMOUS} BĚLLY# – – –
            A: (M̀))# – – –
            B: **how do you get ÒN with {THÒRPE#}#**
               (1.6:654–75)

And the speakers go on to talk about Thorpe's lecturing
commitments and, not least, his dynamic personality.

> **Return markers:**
> all right
> right
> OK
> (well) now
> now then
> anyway
> so

Making an aside

> An **aside** is an utterance that is not integrated in the conversation

The extract below is from a legal examination. The judge turns to one of the counsels for information concerning a medical <statement>:

> [364] C: is it DÁTED {Mr SMÍTH#}# . . . is it DÁTED#
> A: NÒ milord# it ÌSN'T# – it is not . DÀTED#
> (11.1:501–06)

Although the aside is closely connected with the ongoing examination, it does constitute a breakaway from the actual questioning. On the other hand, the information is relevant for the outcome of the examination.

Speech-in-action

> **Speech-in-action** is extra-topical talk which is embedded in the conversation

The instances of speech-in-action met with in the Corpus consist of inquiries about time and date, offers of food and drink, and accompanying talk:

> [365] A: . . . I lose MÓRE# IMMÉDIATELY# then MÀLLET
> does# . although less . perhaps in the LÒNG
> term#

> B: **have a glass of SHÉRRY#** .
> A: **ÒH# that's NÍCE of you# as I'm not**
> **DRÍVING# . THÀNK you#**
> B: **bloody HÈLL# – – –**

> A: but what about YÒU# ə CRÌSPIN# . . .
> (1.2:838–50)

The offering of a glass of sherry has obviously no connection whatsoever with the conversation as such, but it is certainly part of the speech situation and has an important social effect. The reason for the <exclaim> is probably that B spilt some of the sherry.

Summing up how to deal with topics

In a conversation the speakers talk about one or more topics, which in their turn may consist of one or more subtopics. Casual conversation is characterized by topic drifts, ie unnoticeable transitions from one topic to the next by association.

Topic change, which involves going from one topic to a new and unrelated topic, is generally marked by a transition marker, and so are topic shifts, ie the transition between related topics. <Frames>, <prefaces>, <metacomments>, tempo variations, pauses, and laughter serve as transition markers.

▶▶▶▶▶ **Now try this!**

sŎ *there we* ÀRE serves as a boundary marker. Does it terminate a topic, or does it introduce a new topic, or does it do both?

> A: . . . and she said ((Malcolm had arrived at this new FLĂT))# which is a long way for me to GŎ#
> B: M̆# –
> A: sŎ# there we ÀRE# –do you LĬKE this work HÉRE# . in this DEPÁRTMENT# (1.6:127–33)

[Suggested answer on p 217]

How to close a conversation

Most closing sections consist of winding-up talk and polite phrases before the conversation is definitely called off and closed. Closing a face-to-face conversation may be more demanding than closing a telephone call, the main reason being that telephone closings are rather routine-like, while the face-to-face situation may demand more varied closing techniques.

Face-to-face closings

A distinction has been made between informal and formal face-to-face openings (p 140). The same distinction will be used for closings.

Informal conversation
In the normal case a visitor initiates the closing when leaving:

[366a] **at home**
A: **((that)) REMÌNDS me#** I'm GÒING# (1.9:512–13)

Some winding-up talk follows and A makes up her mind and thanks, but she leaves without saying goodbye:

[366b] A: RÌGHT# . ((bye))BỲE# THÀNK you#
B: ə (coughs –) THÀNKS ((2 sylls))#
c: pardon
B: THÀNK you# – *for the SHÈRRY#* –
c: *(laughs –)* a great pleasure Dai (1.9:542–49)

In the odd case it is not the visitor who takes the initative but the other party:

[367a] **at work**
A: ... **what time is your** – BÒAT train# or *whatever it*
B: *PLÀNE#* (3.2:717–19)

New talk may follow, before the visitor initiates the final closing sequence:

[367b] B: WÈLL then# THÀNKS for the CÓFFEE#
A: great PLÉASURE# glad to SÈE you# BỲE#
B: BỲE# (3.2:737–41)

Formal conversation
This closing from the end of an academic interview (cf pp 177–80) is a typical example of how a formal conversation is closed. It turns out to be a stepwise procedure. The interviewee, ie the leaver, takes the first step:

[368a] step 1
A: **well** can you give me any FÙRTHER help then# I'm SÒRRY# I'm holding up your TÌME# (3.1:551–53)

A few comments follow, and the interviewee realizes that her time is up:

[368b] step 2
A: **all RÍGHT# – THÀNK you#** (3.1:567)

At this point one of the interviewers remembers to ask for the interviewee's essay, and the other interviewer closes the session:

[368c] step 3
B: **RÍGHT# – GOOD*BÝE#***
A: ***GOOD*BÝE#** (3.1:572–74)

The closing section is brief, matter-of-fact and polite. There is no 'extra' talk other than what the situation demands.

Telephone closings

Telephone closings, like telephone openings, differ in complexity and formality depending on who calls whom and under what circumstances, but in any case it is generally the caller who takes the initiative. Closings are typically initiated by *right*, *alright* and *OK*.

The categories described earlier in this chapter (p 143) for openings, repeated here for the sake of convenience, are terminated as follows. 'Calls answered by a telephonist' are not interesting in this context, since the closing involves a second answerer.

[369] **answered by secretary**
A: HELLÓ#
B: HELL=O# ə:m ə:m is that Babcock WÒRTH'S ə: SÉCRETARY#

B: . . . OḰ#
A: RÍGHT# *thanks very MÚCH#*
B: *((2 sylls))* BÝE# (9.1:272–75)

The caller initiates the closing (OḰ) and has the last word: (BÝE).

[370] **answered by person in charge**
A: SÉWING-machine centre# good AFTERNÒON#
B: good AFTERNÒON# – ə:m do you stock NÈCCHI MACHÍNES#

B: . . . OK̇# **thank you** very MÙCH#
A: RÍGHT#
B: **RÌGHT#** **GOODBYÈ#**
A: *((2 sylls))* (8.1:616–20)

The caller initiates the closing section (OK̇) and the farewell exchange. The answerer has the last word, although exactly what he says happens to be difficult to figure out.

[371] answered by individual at work

A: EXTÈNSION five |əu| TWÓ#
B: (. giggles HELLÓ# .
A: HELLȮ#
B: HÌ# .
A: how are YÒU#

B: M̀# . **I must GÒ#** – –
A: SȮ# see you next WÈEK#
B: MHM *ALL RÍGHT#*
A: *BỲE#*
B: bye BỲE#
A: SÈE you#
B: see YÓU# (7.2:892–901)

The caller initiates the closing (*I must GÒ*). The answerer initiates the farewell exchange, and the caller has the last word.

[372] answered by individual at home

A: seven one seven NÍNE# .
B: JÈAN# .
A: oh HULLÓ Annie#

B: **RÌGHT#** . *have a nice WEEKÉND#*
A: *((don't know when I shall)) be ÍN but . . . . . .

B: RÍGHT# OK̇# .
A: =OK̇# THÁNKS Annie# have a nice WEEKÉND#
B: and YÓU# .
A: GOODBÝE#
B: **BÝE#** (7.2:200–07)

The caller initiates the closing (R Ì GHT), which turns into a 'pre-closing', since the answerer starts new talk. A final closing is initiated, again by the caller, who also has the last word (BÝE).

Summing up closings

Face-to-face and telephone closings have at least the following general characteristics in common:

- the adjacency-pair format for pre-closings, closings, <thanks> and goodbyes
- the visitor/caller usually initiates the closing section and the goodbye exchange
- items like *right*, *alright* and *OK* (and *thanks*) figure in both

The extracts from the face-to-face and telephone conversations exemplified do not correspond entirely to this pattern, however, which shows very clearly that there are plenty of exceptions when it comes to details.

▶▶▶▶ **Now try this!**

Can you identify the following closings? Which of them are telephone closings, for instance?

[a] B: well thank you SÒ much {IND=EED#}# for your
     TÍME#
  a: nice to see you
  B: BÝE BÝE#
  a: bye (2.1:1156–60)

[b] B: OḰ feller# SÈE you#
  A: BÝE bye ÉDGAR# THÀNKS# (9.2:1164–67)

[c] B: THÀNKS for the CÓFFEE#
  A: great PLÉASURE# glad to SÈE you#BÝE#
  B: BÝE# (3.2:737–41)

[d] B: ÓK#
  A: all RÍGHT#
  B: GOODBÝE Mr Gerrymander#
  A: bye BÝE# (8.3:491–94)

[Answer on p 217]

Summing up conversational strategies

The following can be concluded about face-to-face conversations and telephone calls in general:

Face-to-face conversations:

- opening and closing sections may be lacking
- openings and closings are affected by the degree of formality
- topic changes, shifts and drifts are common (cf pp 154–8)
- body language plays an important role
- extralinguistic details play an important role (eg the fact that a conversation takes place in a university department)

Telephone calls:

- there is always an opening, followed by a reason for calling and a closing
- openings and closings contain a minimal set of obligatory actions
- extralinguistic features (except laughters, sighs and the like) play no role

Closings and farewells have their typical realizations:

<Call-offs> Speaker A:		<Closers> Speaker B:
all RÍGHT	<--------------------->	all RÌGHT
OḰ	<--------------------->	OḰ (then)
OK THÉN	<--------------------->	see you THÉN
OḰ	<--------------------->	RÌGHT you ÁRE
RÍGHT	<--------------------->	RÌGHT
right you ÀRE	<--------------------->	RÌGHT
so LÓNG	<--------------------->	ta TÁ
THÀNKS (a lot)	<--------------------->	RÌGHT
thanks a LÒT	<--------------------->	RÌGHT
thanks very much INDÈED	<------>	THÀNK you
thank you SÒ much for your TÍME		nice to see you
we'll see you SÒON	<------------>	that's ÍT
look forward to SÈEING you	<--->	all RÌGHT

```
┌──────────────────────────────────────────────────────────┐
│ 1st farewells              2nd farewells                 │
│ Speaker A:                 Speaker B:                    │
│                                                          │
│ SÉE you  <──────────────────────>  see YÓU             │
│ SÉE you  <──────────────────────>  YÈAH                 │
│ bye BÝE  <──────────────────────>  RÌGHT (BÝE)         │
│ bye BÝE  <──────────────────────>  bye BÝE             │
│ bye BÝE  <──────────────────────>  OḰ BÝE              │
│ good BÝE <──────────────────────>  bye BỲE            │
└──────────────────────────────────────────────────────────┘
```

▶▶▶▶▶ **Now try this!**

How would you describe the structure of this telephone call? (It is not the entire call; most of the message section is missing.)

> a: hello Ann it's Joan
> B: HELLÒ {JÒAN#}#
> a: (sings Happy Birthday)
> B: THÁNK you# (– laughs) I DÌD have {a nice BÌRTHDAY#}#
> a: you did
> B: yes THÁNK you# ((it was LÒVELY))#
> a: oh good – what happened
> B: oh nothing HÁPPENED# ((I don't KNÒW))# I left WÓRK# and everybody was very NÍCE to me# and I got a nice PRÉSENT and everything#
> a: what did you get – –
> B: ah they GÁVE me# a very nice WRÍTING case# əm a sort of white plastic CÓVERED thing# (7.1:1165–72)
>
> (story continues)
>
> B: all RÍGHT# – –
> a: right then
> B: that's FÍNE# did you have a nice WEEKÊND#
> a: oh it was all right it was dull – you know . ə I mean let's face it there's nothing to do in Wimslow at all – – but not to worry I shall tell you all about it tomorrow my love
> B: all RÍGHT# . I'll see you at half past TWÈLVE#
> a: half past twelve *out*side the dome
> B: *OK#* – YÈAH# . *RÍGHT#*
> a: *OK* then

B: bye BYE#
a: bye bye (7.1:1370–83)

[Suggested answer on p 217]

Types of talk

The following categories of spoken interaction will be described in terms of overall framework, topical development, and interactional structure and strategies:

$$\text{SPOKEN INTERACTION} \begin{cases} \text{interviews} \\ \text{discussions} \\ \text{conversations} \end{cases}$$

In order to facilitate the description I have decided to go from the most to the least rule-bound type of interaction. Great emphasis will be placed on the topical development. Remember that the transaction, the highest of the five levels in the discourse hierarchy, corresponds to one topic in the topical structure (cf p 30) and that the next lower discourse unit is the exchange where the information is negotiated.

Interviews

Interviews are always carried out for a particular **purpose** and in a special **setting**. An admissions interview conducted in a university department, a radio-broadcast political interview, and a courtroom examination will be compared.

Interviews are different from both discussions and conversations in that the 'second turn' is of particular importance. It is what the interviewee says that is most interesting. A description of interviews must therefore pay special attention to the [response].

A legal cross-examination

Setting: Courtroom
Speakers: **A** male counsel, 65
           B male plaintiff, c 50
           C male judge, 64

D male counsel, 26
Topic: The signing of a will

The examination concerns a civil case regarding the signing of a will. It is partly a recapitulation of the previous day's examination. Four persons are directly involved in the proceedings, but counsel A and plaintiff B are the main actors. In the extract that follows the parties have come to a point where the plaintiff is asked to specify exactly what happened when his mother signed her will. The crucial question is whether she had had too much to drink when she did it:

[373] A: Mr P=OTTER# did YÒU# – – ARRÍVE# about
two O'CLÒCK# on |ði| . SÙNDAY# . **the date
the will was . SÌGNED#** .
B: YÉS# – –
A: and . did you . GÓ# and see your mother straight
AWÁY#
B: YÈS I did#
A: what was she then DÒING# .
B: she was having her LÙNCH# – – –
A: **what about the BRÀNDY bottle# where was
THÀT#** – –
B: I don't KNÒW# (11.1:1–15)

And counsel continues the interrogation, typically going from the more general to the more specific:

[374] A: **how did she SÈEM {THÈN#}#** – ((at)) two
O'CLÒCK# –
B: WÉLL# . she seemed all RÍGHT# . . .

A: did she – – RÈAD# . NÓRMALLY# or did she
require ASSÍSTANCE {in RÈADING#}# .
B: she ÚSED a MÀGNIFYING {GLÀSS {to
RÈAD#}#]# . (11.1:24–70)

Not only the son, Mr Potter, but also the mother's doctor played an important role. At this point the judge takes over the interrogation:

[375] C: did she telephone ÁNYBODY#
B: NÒ . {my LÒRD#}# – – –
A: **did you TÉLEPHONE {the DÓCTOR#}#** (11.1:
351–53)

The examination concentrates on the mother's physical and mental condition. Notice the skilful narrowing down:

> [376] A: that's your mother's HÀND-WRITING# ÌSN'T
> it#
> B: yes it ÍS# .
> A: a fair SÁMPLE# of it# .
> B: YÉS# – –
> A: a strong firm HÀND# – –
> B: YÉS#
> A: can you ACCÒUNT# for the FÀCT# that |ði|
> signatures on the WÌLLS# the FÌVE SÍGNATURES#
> – are so SHÀKY# (11.1: 1001–12)

This sequence is characteristic:

> [377] A: did you know mother had been DRÌNKING# –
> B: I DÒN'T think# mother had been drinking at
> ÀLL# .
>
> A: did she drink . when YǑU were there# – –
> B: NÓ# she did NÒT# –
>
> A: are you SÚRE#
> B: I'm absolutely PÒSITIVE#
> A: very GÒOD# – – – (11.1:144–58)

The examination goes on along the following lines, until enough facts have been confirmed (see p 172).

Overall framework
This type of talk takes place within a routine-like, largely pre-scheduled framework. All those involved have fixed roles; the way the examination is conducted is largely pre-established; a large part of what is done in the examination is done in terms of <questions> and <answers>; and who asks the <questions> and who answers is determined beforehand. Not surprisingly, in this very formal situation there is no laughter.

Owing to the situation, digressions are avoided, but the questioning sequences are broken up in places by an aside consisting of the judge's and counsel's supplementary deliberation. The overall pattern is questioning, responding and summing up.

One feature typical of the court-room is the use of

TOPICS

ASIDES

A: did you KNÒW# mother had been DRÌNKING# ...

— —
C: well I'm —now in great DÌFFICULTY# MILÒRD#

C: well I'd like to know what you're SÀYING about THÍS# . are you SÀYING# that ə . the doctor's RECOLLÈCTION# was completely WRÓNG# ...

A: — — — you SÈE# I SUGGÈST# — Mr PÓTTER# quite PLÁINLY# that . your MÒTHER# telephoned the DÒCTOR# ...

A: |ði| STÁTEMENT# . of the DÒC- TOR# .... did you SÉE it# ...

C: is it DÁTED [Mr SMÍTH#]#

A: well NÓW# — — — the document you have in FRÒNT of you# ... had you SÈEN that# ...

A: W=ELL# . (. coughs) no doubt |ði| . my LǑRD will have the exact words of the DÒCTOR# ...

A: WÈLL# . you say several PÉOPLE# . who was in the HÒUSE# apart from you and your WÌFE# — ...

A: just look at the — — ÈARLIER {PÀRAGRAPH#}# extracted from your STÁTEMENT# — ...

honorifics. The plaintiff and counsels are addressed by *Mr* plus second name, while the judge is addressed as *milord* by the plaintiff and as *your lordship* by the two counsels.

Topical development

The very first questioning sequence is introduced by counsel who addresses the plaintiff by *Mr P=OTTER*. Otherwise, new sequences are either preceded by a long pause or marked off by a <frame>, NÒW, *well* NÒW. The same refers to summing-ups. Asides are preceded by a long pause, eg – – – *what do you* SÀY {*Mr HÒOKER#*}#.

Since a legal cross-examination is by definition a goal-directed activity, the questioning procedure progresses relentlessly until enough facts have been gathered and confirmed.

Interactional structure and strategies

The whole examination constitutes a transaction, with a long series of questioning sequences, which alternate with summing-up sequences and lead up to a final conclusion. The questioning sequences consist of <question>-<answer>-(<evaluate>) exchanges, while the summing-up sequences usually consist of <inform>-<reply> exchanges.

Counsel A conducts the examination, but his role is sometimes taken over by the judge for clarification and confirmation. The plaintiff, B, answers <questions> and replies to counsel A's 'suggestions' in the summing-ups. Besides taking over the examination in places, the judge deliberates with A and asks counsel D (who acts as an assistant) for additional information.

The form of a great number of <questions> reveal their purpose, which consists in making the respondent agree to and confirm whatever is put forward to him. The number of 'leading' and 'concluding' <questions> far exceeds the number of 'genuine' <questions>.

One typical questioning technique consists in the counsel's initiating a sequence of <questions> by what looks like an <information request> and continuing by a series of <questions> disguised as <confirmation requests>. A second technique consists in narrowing down the <questions>, as if to trap the respondent.

TYPICAL FEATURES

Boundary markers: *now, well now, Mr Potter*
Turntakers: *and, no, so, well, yes*

[Backchannels]:   –
<Empathizers>:   *you see*
Exchange patterns: I<question>
R<answer>
(F<evaluate>)

I<state>
R<reply>

A political radio interview

Setting: Studio
Speakers: **a** male broadcaster, 43
b male politician, c 60
Topic: Governmental policy

A former British Prime Minister is interviewed by a radio reporter. The situation is very special in that there is an audience but the speakers and the audience cannot see each other. This puts extra pressure on both interviewer and interviewee to be clear and exhaustive. The interview begins as follows:

[378] A: Prime MÌNISTER# W=E – read in the NEWS-
PÁPERS# that Mr Heath's putting on WEÍGHT# .
and that . you've been getting some of your SÙITS
taken in# –

you're not – lying AWÀKE at night# worrying
about the date of the next ELÈCTION# ÁRE you#
(6.3:1–7)

Notice how the reporter only gradually arrives at the point. The same refers to nearly all the <questions> in the interview. The [focus] move prepares the way for the next issue, eg by giving necessary background information or placing the <question> in the right context. Clearly, the introductory [focus] move is of particular importance in a situation like this where there is a third party who cannot ask for clarification. This is another example:

[379] A: let me bring you . |k| quickly back to ÈUROPE
Prime Minister# |ði| . the tone of the speech Mr
CÀLLAGHAN made . {this WÈEK}# . struck many
PÉOPLE# as . notably more ACCÒMMODATING than
his FÍRST# – RENEGOTIÁTION speech on April the
FÍRST# –

does that reflect a . shift of INTÉNTION# . *on your
government's PÀRT#* (6.3:878–85)

<Answers> are generally extremely long, judging by conversa-
tional standards. One gets the impression that the Prime Minister is
allowed to go on as long as he likes. The following <answer> is a
much shortened version of the <answer> to the <question> above:

[380] b: *not at ÀLL# the IN*TÈNTION is the SÁME# it's . it
was the SÁME# – ((and)) it has BÈEN the SÁME#
with ə: |ði| CÁBINET# with MYSÉLF# – – ə from
nineteen sixty-SÉVEN#
. . .

and ə Mr CÁLLAGHAN# was CONCÈRNED# to
make these points very clear in his STÀTEMENT#
with the full AUTHÓRITY# – of the CÀBINET#
(6.3:886–944)

Sometimes the <answer> goes far beyond the <question> by
providing much more information than was asked for; sometimes it
deviates slightly from the <question> and does not really answer it.
However, it is up to the interviewer to see to it that the interviewee
follows the rules of the game:

[381] a: tick ÒFF FÒR me# |ði:| . the {MÀIN} THÌNGS#
that you would . you would claim to have ACHÌ-
EVED . {as a GÒVERNMENT#} . {since the ELÈC-
TION#}# (6.3:118–21)

The interview continues along the following lines (see p 176):

Overall framework
After a somewhat informal beginning with a reference to the Prime
Minister's loss of weight as a consequence of the approaching
election, the interview concentrates on one main topic, 'the
government's policy'. This main topic is discussed in terms of six
different but related issues, ie subtopics. The pattern is neat and
regular, with no digressions, asides or instances of speech-in-action.

Topical development
All the topics are introduced in the same way, by a fairly long
preparatory [focus] move and a <question>, where the issue to be
discussed is highlighted. And a very long <answer> follows. The

TOPICS

a: nineteen sixty-FÒUR# lies quite a long way in the PÀST now
. . .

what would you claim to have ACHÌEVED

a: could we for the M=OMENT# – go across . . . to . to
ÍRELAND#

would you CONCÈDE that it was . . .

a: events in ÌRELAND# have tended to distract attention from
the state of the ECÒNOMY# in the CÒUNTRY# as a
WHÒLE# –

I wonder if I could get you to think ALÒUD a little about the
ideal of a social CÒNTRACT#

a: you mentioned the MANIFÉSTO# . . .

how does that square with increases . . .

a: by the ÀUTUMN Prime MÍNISTER# you'll have to have
something to put in the place of the Conservative Phase
THRÈE#

how is your GÒVERNMENT'S MÍND# MÒVING on that at the
moment#

a: you went to the SCÌLLY Isles# . . .

I WÔNDER# if you saw a REPÒRT#. . . how do you FÈEL
about {THÀT#}#

a: you've frequently SÁID# that a final decision . ÒN ÉUROPE#
must be made . through the BÀLLOT-BÓX# . . .

would it suit your purpose BÈTTER . . .

a: one or two questions about FÓREIGN affairs Prime Minister#
. . .

do you think they have a PÓINT# . . .

[focus] serves as transition marker. Another marker to be noticed is the honorific 'Prime Minister'. This address term is used on several occasions when a new aspect is brought up for discussion.

The fact that the subtopics are closely related is reflected, for instance, in the transition from 'the Irish question' to 'British economy': *events in ÌRELAND . . . ECÒNOMY# in the CÒUN-TRY# as a WHÒLE#.*

Interactional structure and strategies

The entire interview can be characterized as one long transaction consisting of a sequence of exchanges, each of which constitutes one subtopic (or aspect within a subtopic). The exchange pattern is [Focus] [Initiate] [Response].

The reporter asks all the <questions>, and the Prime Minister provides all the <answers>. Although all the <answers> are very long, the reporter never manifests that he is paying attention by inserting [backchannels], either verbal or in the form of laughter. Silent pauses, even if they are long, are never taken advantage of by the other party. Hesitation markers other than pauses are rare.

TYPICAL FEATURES

Boundary markers: [Focus<preface>]
Turntakers: –
Backchannels: –
Empathizers: –
Exchange pattern: Focus<preface>
                       I<question>
                       R<answer>

An academic interview

Setting: Office in a university department
Speakers: **a** male academic, c 40
               A female prospective undergraduate, c 20
               B male academic, c 40
Topic: A's qualifications

Mrs Finney, speaker A, wants to go back to university and do an honours course in English. Two male university teachers, a and B, conduct an interview to find out whether she has adequate qualifications. This is the way it opens:

[382] a: come in . come in − − ah good morning
A: good MÒRNING#
a: you're Mrs Finney
A: Y=ES# I ÀM#
a: how are you − my name's Hart and this is Mr
Mortlake
B: ((how *are YÒU))#*
A: *((HÒW do you* do))# .
a: ə: won't you sit down
A: THÀNK you# − − (3.1:1–12)

After the rather formal opening the interview can begin. (see p 179)

Overall framework
The interview consists of an opening, a section where preliminaries are discussed, the interview proper, a conclusion, and a closing. The interview proceeds without disturbances in the form of digressions and asides. The two occurrences of speech-in-action concern Mrs Finney's essay and are similar to stage directions. The atmosphere can be characterized as polite and friendly but tense.

Topical development
All the sections are properly marked by boundary markers, the preliminary section (ə:m − well), the interview (well now), the conclusion (well look . ə honestly) and the closing section (all R Í GHT). There is a steady progression until the bitter end where it turns out that Mrs Finney does not possess the adequate knowledge and is refused admission.

Interactive structure and strategies
Certain characteristics stand out. First, the interview proper consists of nothing but <questions> and <answers>; the interviewers ask all the questions, and the applicant provides all the <answers>. Second, the <answers> are generally followed by an evaluating [follow-up] move; the exchange pattern is [Initiate] [Response] [Follow-up]. Third, the large majority of <questions> are <information requests> (realized by *WH-* and *yes/no-* interrogatives). Fourth, both interviewer and interviewee use *well* and the filled pause *ə:m*, which means that these items occur in both <questions> and <answers>. *ə:m* indicates hesitation in both cases; *well* is used either as a <starter> or as a hesitation marker, <staller>.

The fact that Mrs Finney is faced with a difficult <question> is reflected in nervous laughter and long silent pauses and in

TOPICS   SPEECH-IN-ACTION

a: **ə:m – well** you are . proposing
. taking on . quite something

B: and do you know anything
about the CÓNTENT {of an
English   HÒNOURS   course
here#}#

a: you were accepted here once
before . . .

a: **well now** to come back to your
reading

                                            a: ə:m your essay if I
a: ə:m – – ə we'd like you to   may cut across
re-read this little passage

a: but you haven't written much
in the time have you

a: what reading have you done to
show that you are interested in
English literature

a: **well look** . ə **honestly Mrs
Finney** ə: my suggestion . . .

a: well what your best bet is to go
to the University Library

A: **well** can you give me any
FÙRTHER help then#

A: **all RÍGHT#** – THÀNK you# . . .   a: could we have your .
B: RÌGHT# – GOODBÝE#   essay back please

reformulations and cut-off sentences. The following <answer> reflects her predicament:

> [383] a: what are your reservations here
> A: ə:m – – oh I oh DEÀR# . NÒW# . let me SÈE# – – – well . . . (3.3:189–93)

Finally, she uses *you know* as an <appealer> for sympathy rather than as an 'ordinary' social marker.

TYPICAL FEATURES
Boundary markers: ə:*m, well, well now, all right*
Turntakers: *yes, well*
[Backchannels]:   –
<Empathizers>:   *you know*

Typical exchange pattern: I<question>
                                  R<answer>
                                  F<evaluate>

Summing up interviews

Interviews are characterized by the following general features:

- they are goal-directed
- they follow a set pattern
- the types of obligatory move that occur are predetermined: [Initiate<question>] and [Response<answer>]
- optional moves (depending on the type of dialogue) are: [Focus<preface>] and [Follow-up<evaluate>]
- who does what is predetermined: the interviewer asks the <questions> and the interviewee provides the <answers>

The interviews described here differ, for instance, in the following respects:

- <question> **form**: declaratives and tag-questions dominated in the legal examination as opposed to *WH-* and *yes/no-* interrogatives in the academic interview, while the <questions> in the radio interview were usually introduced by a [focus] move;
- <answer> **form**: short <answers> dominated in the legal interview; although the <questions> in the academic

interview invited exhaustive <answers>, the length depended on the interviewee's knowledge; all the <answers> in the radio interview were long and exhaustive.

▶▶▶▶ **Now try this!**

This extract is characteristic of the legal examination exemplified above. What kind of 'interview' technique is used?

A: WÈLL# Captain and Mrs KÁY# lived in a . FLÀT# on their ÒWN#

B: Y=ES# .

A: and they didn't CÓME down# until . after TÈA# DÌD they#

B: NÓ# .

A: some time between tea and CHÙRCH# .

B: Y=ES#

A: S=O# (. coughs) – there's only . ÉLSIE# and your WÌFE#

B: YÉS# – – – (11.1:677–91)

[Answer on p 217]

Discussions

Discussions can be expected to be fairly strict when it comes to the distribution of speaker roles, the allocation of speaker turns, and the form of the individual speakers' contributions. The character of discussions varies, however, depending on what is being discussed, who the participants are and under what circumstances the discussion takes place. There is no homogeneous pattern for all types. A radio discussion and a committee meeting will be compared.

A radio discussion

Setting: Studio
Speakers: **A** male radio producer, 53
              B retired lawyer, 95 (father of **A**)
              C female 24 (daughter of **A**)
Topics: Generation gaps, sex relations

Three persons take part in a radio discussion on 'generation gaps' arranged by a male radio producer (A), who has brought his father

(B) and his daughter Lizzy (C) to the studio. He begins by introducing the guests:

> [384] A: W=ELL# I've brought us – . TO{GÈTHER} ĬN the
> studio# cos I think there ÀRE# . really rather
> UN{ĬQUE} ÈLEMENTS# ĬN our relationship#
> |ə:n| one of the things ĬS {I THĬNK#}# |ði:| . gap
> between our ÀGES# ə: GR=AMPY# . (6.4:1–8)

After a few comments on the age gap 'Grampy' says:

> [385] B: well I I of course was BŎRN# NINETY-FĬVE years
> ago# . |i| I was the GRÀNDSON# . ə ə of |ði ði|
> great PÒET# . who was in FÀCT# . one of the
> THRÈE# . leading PERSONÀLITIES# of the Anglo
> |s| ə of the Anglo-Saxon WÒRLD# . at the TĬME#
> . (6.4:34–42)

He then gives a brief account of his childhood and early education. We learn that he went to Eton and Cambridge, that he went into law and business and that he retired 27 years ago.

When Lizzy's turn comes, she begins by addressing her grandfather:

> [386] C: well it's quite SIGNIFĬCANT# that I've only
> KNŎWN you# SĬNCE you've been RETĬRED#
> (6.4:64–66)

We learn that Lizzy was brought up in the country, that she went to a village school and to a 'Direct Grant School', and that she is now working with disturbed children. That terminates the opening.

The discussion begins with Grampy's description of the distant relationship between him and his parents; he lived in the age of nurses when children were only allowed to see their parents at stated periods. This leads on to a few comments on the relationship between father and son and then to the relationship between grandfather and grandchild.

Overall framework
Three steps can be recognized: step one, where speaker A introduces himself and the other two speakers and explains what the discussion is going to be about; step two, where B and C produce a short version of their life story; step three, which constitutes the discussion proper.

The main topic (with several subtopics) is adhered to fairly

TOPICS   DIGRESSIONS

A: ÀCTUALLY# GRÀMPY# there
is one incredible PÒRTRAIT#
of you at about the age of
THRÈE#

A: I {CÈRTAINLY} . FÈEL# much
{CLÒSER in a way to you} than I
did as a CHÌLD#

> B: **I think I ought to
> say something** . . .
> about my STÈP-
> FATHER#
>
> A: ÀCTUALLY#   I
> **think I'd like to
> make a** PÒINT
> **there#** . . .

A: you've been talking about
{YÒUR relationship to} YÒUR
elders# during your YÓUTH#

I wonder how Rozzy sees HÉR
relationship with YÒU#

> A: **I think I must
> make a
> confession#**
> HÈRE# . . .

A: |ði:| way MỲ children# react
TÒ you# must be very DÌFFER-
ENT# from the way YÒU# –
BEHÀVED# to your ÒWN
GRÀNDFATHER . . .

C: **I think** what I think of YÓUR
childhood# in a way makes me
feel a little bit ÈNVIOUS#

B: **I think** |ði:| think which I really
MÌSS from my childhood# is the
{UNSPÒILT} COUNTRYSÌDE#

A: what do you feel about this
QUÈSTION# of the change
in the relations between the
SÈXES#

strictly, thanks to speaker A who is responsible for the programme. Towards the end a somewhat different, but related, topic crops up, 'young people's sex relations'. Digressions occur but are rare. Asides do not occur, and would hardly have been appropriate in the actual situation, nor are there occurrences of speech-in-action.

Topical development

The first topic is gradually drifted into. There is no introductory marker. The second topic, which has a more abrupt start, also lacks a boundary marker. Some of the subtopics are introduced by a [focus] move (eg *you've been talking about* {*YOUR relationship to*} *YOUR elders*), which is certainly very helpful for the listeners. Otherwise, there are occasional <frames> (eg *ACTUALLY*), and <metacomments> (eg *what about*).

Interactional structure and strategies

The transactions, the first of which embraces the main topic and is very long, consist mainly of stating exchanges (I R). Turns are long; the speaker who has the turn is allowed to develop his ideas in full before the next speaker takes over. Grampy, speaker B, does not only talk most but is also the person to whom most of the talk is directed. He pauses a great deal, mainly using filled pauses. The radio producer, speaker A, talks more than his daughter Lizzy, speaker C; he both introduces new aspects and takes part in the discussion.

Lizzy is the only person who produces [backchannels], mainly in the form of laughter. <Empathizers> do not occur at all.

TYPICAL FEATURES
Boundary markers: *actually*
Turntakers: *well, I think,*
[Backchannels]: laughs
<Empathizers>: –
Exchange pattern: [I<inform>]
[R<reply>]

A committee meeting

Setting: Private residence
Speakers: **A** female teacher
B male conductor

C female academic
D male computer specialist
E female academic
F female administrator
G female TV producer
H male civil servant

Topic: Musical standards

Eight committee members have met to discuss the performance of an academic choir. The discussion is opened somewhat awkwardly by A (the female teacher) who has called the meeting. C (the computer specialist) finally manages to ask for a proper agenda:

[387]   A: ə:m . we did . DECÌDE# that we were going to
    have a |pəu| post MÒRTEM# − − −
    D: hang ÓN#
  >A: for the |lau| for |ði:| . Saint Mark's WEEKÈND# − −
    − did we NÒT# − −
    E: M#
  >A: ((and)) that was the ə |ði| ə
    ?: M#
  >A: object of TONÌGHT# − so perhaps RÓY# you
    could ə − − − outline your THÓUGHTS .
    D: could I
  >A: on the matter#
  >D: ask before we do THÀT# − − − can we sort of . map
    out what we actually have to TÁLK about tonight#
    − (5.12:1−16)

The result is an agreement to discuss 'arrangements for the season', including future performances, rehearsals, and fundraising. Speaker A apologizes for her lack of planning before the discussion begins:

[388]   A: ALRÌGHT# ((well)) I'm SÒRRY I haven't pro-
    duced an AGÉNDA# it's very − − . ((LÀX of me))#
    (5.12:53−55)

Overall framework
After the opening deliberations the discussion has one main theme, the musical standards of the academic choir concerned. The discussion proceeds stepwise. First the quality of the most recent performances is discussed, and this serves as a point of departure for step two, ways of improving the quality of future

TOPIC	DIGRESSIONS	SPEECH-IN-ACTION-

A: RÌGHT# —— the Saint Mark's WEEK-ÈND#— the musical —. STÁNDARDS#

B: basically# the Saturday evening concert – was a bit TÀTTY#

B: Sunday MÒRNING# actually# was pretty GÒOD as a WHÓLE# – .

B: – – – ÈVENSONG# – went very NÌCELY# I THÓUGHT#

B: – – . ə:m **well** there are VÀRIOUS factors# . ATTÈND-ANCE {ÀT rehearsals#}# –

B: – **but . I mean** we're NÈVER going to get a rehearsal schedule where we're going to get every-one at every REHÈARSAL#

F: is there not also a practical PRÒBLEM# in that if you have . a rehearsal every WÈEK# – . . .

G: would you **. going going on from . going on from** THÀT# would you be – – terribly opposed# to when when one HÀD a schedule# of of . those more concentrated REHÉ-ARSALS# .

B: can you pass me that

B: **I mean** – just going back to the POST-MÒRTEM for a minute#

A: **so** what conclusion did we come to .

B: there isn't any particular RÈA-SON# why I shouldn't decide decide in advance for the next CÒNCERT#

A: ə:m we should have – – – . a schedule# – .

A: – could you . əm if anybody would like some more

performances. The third step consists in drawing conclusions and making new plans.

The discussion is kept within a comparatively solid framework as far as the content is concerned, with fairly few digressions. Speech-in-action occurs, in particular, towards the end (in the form of offerings of food and drink). There are no asides.

Topical development

Speaker A begins the discussion, using the <frame> (RÌGHT) followed by a long pause to get everybody's attention. The subsequent subtopics are introduced without linguistic markers, with very few exceptions; one is *would you . going going on from . going on from THÀT#* and another *so what conclusion did we come to.* Some digressions, as illustrated on pp 158–9, have a linguistically marked beginning (*I mean – just going back to the POST-MÒRTEM for a minute#*). The parties finally come to a kind of agreement, and the discussion ends with a meal.

Interactional structure and strategies

The entire discussion corresponds to one long transaction. However, with so many people involved, a description of the entire interaction in terms of five neat discourse levels will certainly cause problems.

The atmosphere is relaxed, and even if the speakers keep to the topic they are supposed to discuss, the proceedings are not as orderly as might have been expected. The reason is that nobody acts as chairman, so everybody is free to speak whenever he or she manages to get a word in. This, of course, results not only in simultaneous speech but also in interruptions:

[389] A: . . . the musical – – . STÁNDARDS# – –
      D: (. chuckles *–*)
      B: *well I think we're all AWÀRE* of the . |ði|
           əm# – – RESÙLTS# and ((the)) causes of them#
           – –
      A: WĚLL# *ÁRE we ((aware of the causes))#*
      ?: *m NÒ#*
      ?: NÒ#
      B: *RÌGHT#*
      A: *I think* the causes need ǍNALYSING# *((to be quite honest))#*

B: *NÒ#
  ə* . I wasn't *going to (((several sylls))*
E: *and the RESÙLTS#*
A: *and the RESÙLTS#* . *YÈS#
E: *M̀#*
>B: *((to MÈNTION))# . I* PLÈASE# . interrupt and
  ÀRGUE# — ə:m
A: well we WÌLL#
D: (. chuckles) — — — (5.12:59–79)

The conductor (B) plays the dominant role. Not only does he speak more than the others, he also comes up with more suggestions. The female teacher (A) who called the meeting plays a rather subordinate role. She opens the discussion and she concludes it, but otherwise her contributions are generally reduced to *mhms* and *yeahs*. Only in very few places does she make an effort to 'lead' the discussion:

[390] A: can you . PRÈCIS that {FÓR me#}# (5.12:350)
A: so . ə: what conclusion did we CÓME to#
  (5.12:1030)
A: and then phone BRÌAN WÍLL you# — — (5.12:1073)
A: . . . s=O# — . before the first REHÈARSAL# — — .
  on September the TWENTYFÒURTH# . . . . ə:m]
  — we should have — — . a SCHÈDULE# — .
  (5.12:1076–81)

One of the participants says nothing at all (H) and some say very little (C and E). There is very little laughter. Pauses are frequent, generally functioning as <stallers>. [Backchannels] abound. Speech-in-action occurs in quite a few places, especially towards the end when food is being offered. But there are no asides.

TYPICAL FEATURES

Boundary markers: <metacomments>
Turntakers: ə:m, but, well, I mean, yes, m, no, and, so, I
                           think
[Backchannels[:   yes, m, no
<Empathizers>:   you know
Exchange pattern: I<inform>/opine>
                           R<reply>/object>

Summing up discussions

Although both discussions are goal-directed insofar as the talk circles around one set topic, they differ, for instance, in the following respects:

- the radio discussion is well planned; the committee meeting is not;
- the radio discussion is properly conducted; the committee meeting is not;
- in the radio discussion there is no simultaneous speech; in the committee meeting there is plenty;
- in the radio discussion there are no digressions, asides or instances of speech-in-action; in the committee meeting there are digressions as well as occurrences of speech-in-action;
- the dominating acts in the radio discussion are <informs> and <replies>; the committee meeting contains numerous <opines> and <objects>.

▶▶▶▶▶ **Now try this!**

This extract is from a discussion between a university administrator and staff. In what respect(s) does it seem to differ from the discussions described above?

A: and and and Lew Mastine would be the LÀST person to say# . {NÒTHING} . must be altered in the CÒLLEGE# until this grand plan has DEVÈLOPED# . I mean of CÒURSE we've got to spend a little money# – –

B: CHÀIRMAN# may I raise a *completely DÌFFERENT* point#

A: *YÈAH#* – TÒTALLY different# *RÌGHT#*

B: *we have* suffered for a long WHÌLE# {from} the sense of being rather on the FRÌNGE of things# (3.4:750–60)
[Suggested answer on p 218]

Conversations

Conversation is a social activity involving two or more participants who talk about something. Who they are, how well they know each other, their shared knowledge, and what they are talking about, all is reflected in the language they use and the strategies they adopt. Here, the emphasis is on informal conversation between colleagues and friends.

Two-party and multi-party talk

The general principles governing two-party and multi-party talk are not completely identical, as we shall see. One difference is that two-party conversation requires mutual cooperation, while multi-party talk does not really require everybody to take an active part, another that multi-party talk tends to split into two. In this section we shall examine a dialogue between two academics and a dinner conversation between two married couples.

Two academics talking

Setting: University department
Speakers: **A** female academic, c 45
           B male academic, c 28
Topics: Work, people

B has recently got a job in a university department and is chatting with A, who studied there as an undergraduate and is now doing a thesis with a supervisor from the department. A and B have just met, and A starts the conversation:

> [391a] A: where do YÒU come from# – – .
>   B: ((you mean)) where was I BEFÒRE#
>   A: *YÈS#*
>   B: *((HÌSTORY))#* *(. giggles)*
>   A: *M* –
>   B: IMMÈDIEATELY BEFÒRE# I was teaching in a
>   SCHÒOL . in {ÈGYPT#}# ((but)) before
>   THÁT# I was in ÌNDIA# – (giggles)
>   A: ÒOH# – . ... (1.6:1–12)

B concludes by saying:

> [391b] B: PRÒGRAMMING {COMPÙTERS#}# – *((THÀT'S
>   what Í do))#* (1.6:21–22)

which immediately leads on to:

> [391c] A: *YÈS# do* you know Malcolm BǑWEN# over at
>   the COMPÙTER ÚNIT# (1.6:23–25)

and Malcolm is the topic of conversation for a while.

In the rest of the dialogue the speakers talk about their jobs, colleagues, and former teachers.

Overall framework
We enter the conversation when it has already begun and leave it again before the closing stage. There is one main topic (the university department and people linked to it) and two embedded minor topics (the teacher's training college where A works and B's previous job was). All in all, a great number of subtopics (mostly about people) are covered within the half hour that the conversation lasts. Digressions are frequent.

Topical development
Topic drifts and sudden jumps (apparently unlinked switches) are more common than linguistically marked transitions. Still, the transitions are not altogether unmarked; laughs, giggles and long pauses do the job in most cases.

The main topic is introduced by a <frame> serving as a linguistic boundary marker, SÒ# *there we ÀRE*. The first embedded topic is preceded by laughs and giggles and marked by an expletive, MỲ GÒSH; the second is only preceded by a long pause. The main topic ends with A's concluding remark: *as regards university teachers, they all have their . PECÙLIAR# little QUÍRKS of HUMÀNITY#– – ((YÈS))#*. The embedded topics simply end and a long pause follows. Many of the subtopics seem to be brought up simply to kill a long silence, as if the speakers feel the obligation to go on speaking. Some digressions are introduced by a boundary marker (eg *I REMÈMBER# it isn't quite the same THÍNG*). In other cases digressions seem to be triggered off to avoid a lengthy pause. The resumption of the old topic/subtopic is occasionally marked by a <frame> (eg BÙT# ÀNYWAY#), but more often it is only preceded by pauses and/or laughter.

Interactional structure and strategies
The transactions (three, two of which are embedded) are rather simple. Questioning exchanges, [Initiate] [Response] [Follow-up], and stating exchanges, [Initiate] [Response] predominate. <Questions> introduce (sub)topics more often than <statements> do.

[Backchannels] are not particularly frequent, since active turntaking is the rule. When they occur they are usually realized

TOPICS

DIGRESSIONS

A: SǑ# – there we ÀRE# do you
LÌKE this work HÉRE#

– – –

B: Thorpe's AWÁY is he#

B: – laughs – – – giggles

A: {MỲ} GÒSH# we're a SMÀLL
department#

B: I REMÈMBER# it isn't
quite the same
THÌNG# but a person
when ì was at
SCHÒOL#

A: – – laughs our MÀTHS chap . . .
he's an ÌNDIAN#

A: – – laughs – –
B: I did know one Indian

A: M# – – – where did you
TÈACH#

A: M# – – – what's that
thing that THÒRPE'S
got# sitting on his
DÈSK there#

A: how do you get ÒN with
{THÒRPE#}#

A: . . .SÒME of them here# stand
up poor DÈARS# and haven't
the first CLÙE#

B: giggles – laughs . giggles

A: one we LÒST# Mr CÀRTER#

A: have you ever heard Professor
McCÀLL LÉCTURE#

B: ÎNTERESTING point#
there was a . . .
RÙSSIAN#

by $\grave{M}$, YÈS and, in particular, laughter. Very few <empathizers> are produced.

The role division is interesting. By and large, the female academic (A) brings up the 'main line' topics, while her male colleague (B) is responsible for most of the digressions. The amount of speech produced by each speaker, on the other hand, is roughly equal. The atmosphere is friendly and informal.

TYPICAL FEATURES

Boundary markers: <prefaces>, pauses, laughter
Turntakers: *yes, well, oh*
[Backchannels]: *m/mhm, (oh) really,* laughter
<Empathizers>: *you know*
Exchange patterns: [I<inform>]
[R<reply>/<acknowledge>]

[I<question>]
[R<answer>]
[F<acknowledge>]

A dinner conversation

Setting: Private residence
Speakers: **A** housewife, c 35
B housewife, c 30
C male academic, c 32 (husband of **B**)
D male academic, c 35 (husband of **A**)
Topics: Kitchen equipment, neighbours, Christmas, Pakistani ladies

This conversation takes place shortly before Christmas. A and D have been invited to B and C for a meal. This is how the first topic is introduced:

[392] A: well I must ADMÌT# I feel . I mean Edward's
MÒTHER# and his great . and his GRÀNDFATHER#
B: M̀#
>A: will come ÙP# on Christmas DÁY#
B: ★Y=ES#★
>A: ★but★ I feel SÒMEHOW# . the sheer FÀCT# of not
having to have . to have . this really sort of −− it's for
one thing it does ★NÀRK me# that it's so bloody★
EXPÈNSIVE#
B: ★((10 syllables))★ (4.3:1−10)

This is followed by the first acceptance of an <offer>:

[393] A: shall I take one of ÉACH# while you're HÉRE#
(4.3:44–45) The entire conversation remains within
the 'domestic' world, focusing on housework,
neighbours, Christmas and children.

Overall framework
We are only faced with the message section. Four topics are
discussed: 'buying a freezer', 'neighbours', 'Christmas' and
'Pakistani ladies'. The digressions are few, but the number of
asides is striking. However, considering that nearly all the
instances of speech-in-action consist of offerings of food and
drink, the number is not surprising.

The fact that four persons take part in the conversation is
most obviously reflected in the 'double interaction', or 'split' into
two simultaneous dialogues. Consider the following. A is talking
to B and C is talking to D (asterisks indicating simultaneous
speech have been left out):

[394] B: do you KNÒW# . ((it's)) one thing I HÀTE#
     D: do you do
    >B: Christmas DÌNNER
    >D: your KÌDS# have ((their)) PRÉSENTS## – OVER-
         NÌGHT# ((or something))
     B: I don't like PÒULTRY#
     C: NÒ#
     B: I don't mind CHÌCKEN# or something .
     D: oh we just ((seem to)) give them their STÒCK-
         INGS# and TH=EN# they hand out their
     A: M# – M#
    >D: presents |s| after BRÈAKFAST or something#
    >B: ((minced ÚP))#
     A: M#
    >B: but ((a)) roast . ((PÒULTRY))#
     C: oh Ì see#
     A: M#
    >B: ə: NÀUSEATING# .
     B: and I can manage a CHÌCKEN#
     D: ((m)) well do you go to CHÙRCH or something#
     A: M#

TOPICS	DI-GRESSION	SPEECH-IN-ACTION

B: ((I bought a FRÈEZER

D: did Ĭ drop that#

B: I think she's a SLÀVE to her freezer ...

D: ((what's the TÍME#

it's like the woman BEHÌND who's always got her WASHING out#

A: I'd LÒVE one of THÓSE please

C:- laughs

B: and these two HÒUSES#

B: and these two WÓMEN# have always got loads of WÀSHING out#

c: well have more of THÉSE#

c: wait a MÍNUTE#

A: that is an an is a stupid REMÀRK#

A: I mean we're going to try Christmas Day on a different PÀTTERN#

D: well do you go to CHÙRCH or something#

B: help yourself

D: WÈLL – do you do yours still hang up STÓCKINGS#

c: help YOURSÉLF old boy

ALL:– – – laugh

c: anybody have some more CÒFFEE#

B: now your Pakistani LÁDIES

B: I CÒULDN'T eat anything ÊLSE# . you KNÓW#
C: well we DÔ but# but it DEP{ÈNDS} WHÈN ə:m
B: so I always do a roast CHÌCKEN# (4.3:838–70)

The effect is bewildering, to say the least. But we are misguided by the rendering in print. Those involved in the conversation have apparently no problem in communicating with each other.

Topical development
The first topic is brought up while food is being offered and attention is not paid to it until the serving is done (*you've bought a FRÉEZER# ÒH#*) and terminated by B's concluding remark: *I think she's a SLÀVE to her freezer*, which almost imperceptibly leads over to the next topic: *it's like the woman BEHÌND#*. Topic three is introduced very suddenly, simply because the previous topic has been exhausted, it seems. Laughter marks end of topic. This in turn leads on to topic four after the offering of coffee. Linguistic transition markers between topics are altogether missing.

Subtopics are marked off by the occasional <frame> (*well, now,*). Laughters, like pauses, serve as non-verbal transition markers. Speech-in-action, too, tends to come between (sub)-topics. Topic drifts are typical. No asides occurred.

Interactional structure and strategies
The four transactions are extremely complex in a few places due to simultaneous speech and double interaction. But on the whole, one speaker speaks at a time, and exchanges form reasonably neat transactions. Stating exchanges, [Initiate] [Response], with long initiating moves, are more frequent than questioning exchanges, [Initiate] [Response] [Follow-up], except at (sub)topic begin-nings.

Those who talk most are the ladies (A and B), especially about buying and preparing food. Since speaker C is responsible for the recording, it is not surprising that he remains as much as possible in the background. He offers food (*MÁISIE# ham and . TOMÁTO ((for you))*); he agrees with the current speaker (*M# . THÀT'S the way of P=UTTING it# YÈAH# . M̀#*); he inserts [backchannels]; and he laughs. But he does not really 'say' much.

There is less laughter than in the two-party dialogue. Pauses are comparatively rare. <Empathizers>, both *you know* and *you see*, are used frequently.

TYPICAL FEATURES
Interactional signals: yes, *oh, well, but.*

Turntakers:	*yes, oh, well, I think*
[Backchannels]:	*(oh)yes/yeah/yep, m/mhm, (oh) I see, really,*
	laughter
<Empathizers>:	*you know, you see*
Exchange patterns:	[I<inform>]
	[R<reply><acknowledge>]
	[I<question>]
	[R<answer>]
	([F<acknowledge>])

Summing of conversations

The participation of more than two speakers affects:

- the overall structure: the conversation may split into two;
- the exchange pattern: more than one speaker can respond, ask for clarification, and so on;
- the turntaking: it may be difficult to get a word in; some speakers participate mainly by backchannelling; simultaneous speech is frequent.

▶▶▶▶ **Now try this!**

What, other than the topic for discussion, indicates that this (abbreviated) extract is taken from an informal chat?

B: we had ((some)) NÍPS to dinner the other NÍGHT# at a frightfully posh bank DÍNNER-PARTY# and in the ÉND# everybody started doing THÌS {with CHÈR-RIES#}# – and it livened ÙP {TÈRRIBLY#}#

C: I'd+ do it very WÈLL#

d: it's very difficult

B: YÈS# TÈRRIBLY difficult# . *((TRÝ))#*

C: I don't *think* you're allowed to *SÙCK {ÈITHER#}#* . I think that's CHÈATING#*

d: *((I'll try again – like that))* (. sniffs) you put the end in your *mouth*

A: *((there's))* {NÒ} WÀY of *doing it#*

C: *((no ÒUT))#*

B: the only way you can DÒ it# is by sticking your tongue out to BEGÍN with# and getting your tongue DRÝ# – and then LÍCKING it up with your TÒNGUE# – – – very HÁRD# ÌSN'T it#

C: =M#
A: CÒR# you don't half look *STÙPID# ÀLL of you#*
C: *don't PÙT your . * HÈAD back# – – –
B: not ÉASY# ÍS it#–
C: THÈN# CÀN you# while it's in your MÓUTH# bite the
CHÈRRY ÓFF# – and then spit {ÒUT} the stone still
connected to the STÀLK# (2.10:1281–1330)

[Suggested answer on p 218]

Summing up types of talk

Some of the features that characterize the different types of
talk are the following:

CHARACTERISTICS	INTERVIEW	DISCUSSION	CONVERSATION
what parties 'do' is predetermined	+		
who talks when is predetermined	+		
it contains phatic talk	+		+
it contains asides	+		+
it is goal-directed	+	+	
it is cooperative	+	+	+
it contains signals and markers	+	+	+
it contains simultaneous speech		+	+
it contains [backchannels]		+	+
it contains digressions		+	+
it contains speech-in-action		+	+
it is 'social'			+

Judging by this figure, which is both a generalization and a
simplification, two features characterize all three types of talk,
cooperativeness and the use of signals and markers. Phatic talk,
which is typical of conversation, occurs in certain kinds of
interviews, but not usually in discussions. The same refers to
asides. Otherwise, discussions have more in common with
conversations than with interviews. Interviews and conversations
are very different; whereas interviews follow a rigorous pattern
when it comes to what parties are allowed to do and who is
allowed to speak when, there are no such restrictions in ordinary
conversation.

If you want to know more:

on conversational structure, see Atkinson and Heritage (eds) (1984),
    Button and Lee (eds) (1987), Coulmas (ed) (1981), Goodwin
    (1981), McLaughlin (1984), McTear (1979);
on telephone openings, see Hopper (1989), Schegloff (1968);
on telephone closings, see Schegloff and Sacks (1973);
on how to create an atmosphere, see Cheepen (1988) Chs.1,4;
on how to deal with topics, see Bublitz (1988), Button and Casey
    (1985), Crow (1983), Jefferson (1987);
on conversational strategies in general, see Brown and Levinson (1978),
    Coulmas (ed) (1981), Fairclough (1989) Ch.3, Fox (1987),
    Goffman (1979), Labov and Fanshel (1977), Richards and Schmidt
    (1983), Thomas (1985), Watts et al (eds) (1992), Wilson (1990);
on interviews, see Atkinson (1984), Atkinson and Drew (1979),
    Cheepen (1988) Ch.3, Goodrich (1987);
on two-party and multi-party talk, see Ellis and McClintock (1990),
    Mandelbaum (1979), Tannen (1986, 1989, 1990).

CHAPTER 5
Discourse and grammar

Although the grammatical description of language is based on its
written form, the grammatical correspondence between the two
modes of expression is bound to be much greater than the
difference, given that the spoken language gave rise to the written
form.

The prosodic chunking of speech into tone units, and to
some extent pause units, is reflected in the syntactic chunking
into clauses, phrases and words. At the level of discourse, moves
and acts might also be described in terms of syntactic units.

The turn is the obvious point of departure for this type of
'matching' description, first treated as a stream of speech
segmented into pause units and tone units, and second, as a rank
in the discourse hierarchy consisting of moves and acts.

What's in a turn?

Do we really speak in sentences? The answer is both 'yes' and
'no'. Many turns are easily analysed in terms of simple,
compound or complex sentences. Other turns consist of only one
word and are not sentence-like at all, while still others far exceed
the structure of one sentence.

A turn can be made up of one of the following syntactic
units:

> a **sentence** consisting minimally of a single clause analysable in terms of S V (O C A) (*it's just FRÌGHTENING#*)
>
> a **clause**: a subclause which cannot (normally) stand alone, (*which is a long bit for me to GŎ#*)
>
> a **phrase** consisting of two or more lexical items (*the academic CŎUNCIL#, in the GÀRAGE#*)
>
> a **word**: a single lexical item (*WĚLL#, G=OOD#, MÁLCOLM#*)

The following alternatives are frequent:

> an **ellipted sentence** with S and/or V missing (*that your WŎLF#*)
>
> a **multiword**: a discourse item consisting of two or more lexical items (*I SĚE#, THÀNK you#, bloody HĚLL#*)
>
> a **combination** of the above units (*ÒH# WĚLL# YÈS#, but . well GRÀCE MÓVED# – [m] PÀRTIALLY because her husband was moving . or NÒT#*)

♣♣♣ the connectors *and*, *but* and *so*, which are used as cohesive ties in written language, are considerably more common as linking devices in spoken language

♣♣♣ the **subordinating** conjunction *because* is often used to initiate a simple sentence, eg in a [response] or a <justify>

Prosodic units

There is a tendency for tone unit boundaries to be accompanied by a silent pause, which seems to indicate that the syntactic content of pause units (pp 203–4) and tone units is the same. They often differ in this respect, however, the main reasons being:

1) that some pause units include more than one tone unit, and
2) that pauses often occur within tone units

Four versions of the same conversational extract will be used as illustration. The extract is from a conversation between three female undergraduates, one of whom is telling the others about a conversation that took place in the senior common room of a women's college that she had just visited.

The first version is a mere orthographic transcription of the running text (1.3:809–26):

> [395a] A: and so we did the eggs everybody made their contribution from all over the senior common-room about their point of view about eggs they were some would rather have them much too soft than much too hard and some people would rather not have an egg at all and some people thought the thing to do was just put them in the water and take them out again and then let them go on cooking without cracking their heads you know you got every possible point of view about boiled eggs then you went on to the next topic

Now imagine that this is a written text with the punctuation missing. A punctuated version is not very difficult to achieve, which only goes to show how close the written language is to the spoken:

	line
[395b] And so we did the eggs .	1
Everybody made their contribution from all	2
over the senior common-room about their	3
point of view about eggs.	4
They were some would rather have them	5
much too soft	6
than much too hard, and some people would	7
rather not have an egg at all.	8
And some people thought the thing to do was	9
just put them in the water and take them out	10
again and then let them go on cooking,	11
without cracking their heads, you know.	12
You got every possible point of view about	13
boiled eggs.	14
Then you went on to the next topic.	15

However, certain features still reveal that this is a spoken text, for instance, the new start in line 5 (*they were some would*), the use of *you know* in line 12, the very simple sentence structure, the frequent use of *and* as a linking device, and the use of generic *you* in lines 13 and 15.

Pause units

If punctuation in writing were a mere reflection of pausing in speech, a brief pause would be expected to separate clauses and a longer pause sentences. This is not the case in our example, however (remember that the dot corresponds to a brief pause, not a period):

		line
[395c] A:	and so we did the eggs .	1
	everybody made their contribution from all	2
	over the senior common-room .	3
	about their point of view about eggs they	4
	were some would rather have them much	5
	too soft than much too hard and some	6
	people would rather not have an egg at all	7
	and –	8
	some people . əm .	9
	thought the thing to do was just put them	10
	in the water and take them out again and	11
	then let them go on cooking without	12
	cracking their heads you know you got	13
	every possible point of view about boiled	14
	eggs –	15
	then .	16
	you went on to the next topic	17

The pauses are few, and the majority are brief. As a matter of fact, there is very little agreement between the faked punctuation in the previous version and the distribution of pauses in the genuine extract.

There are only two pauses that are longer than brief (–), one in line 8 **after** the coordinating conjunction *and*, and one in line 15 marking the end of a complex sentence.

As to brief pauses, the one in line 1 separates simple sentences; the one in line 4 comes before an appended postmodifier; the two brief pauses in line 9 act as <stallers> together with the voiced pause *əm* and the last brief pause, line 16, separates an introductory adverbial from the rest of the sentence.

In sum, although the six sentences in the made-up punctuated version correspond to six pause units, there is not much agreement between syntactic and prosodic units. The six full stops are only matched by two pauses, one of which is brief, and the comma has no matching pause at all. Notice the unit pause (–) after *and*, not before. The comparison indicates that this speaker (at least) does not speak in clauses and sentences but in larger chunks, with no regular division into sentence elements.

Tone units

The next version of the extract is provided with tone unit boundaries and intonation contours (the original tone unit numbering has been changed):

	tone unit
[395d] A: and so we DÌD the eggs# .	1
everybody made their CONTRIBÙ-TION#	2
from all over the senior CÒMMON-ROOM# .	3
about their point of VÌEW about eggs#	4
they ((were)) some would rather have them M=UCH too soft#	5
than much too H=ARD#	6
and some people would rather not have an egg at ÁLL#	7
and – SÒME people# .	8
ə:m . thought ((the THÌNG to do# was))	9
just put them in the water and take them ÒUT again#	10
((and) THÈN let them go on cook-ing#	11
without cracking their HÈADS#	12
you KNÒW#	13
you got every PÒSSIBLE point of VÌEW#	14
about boiled ÈGGS# –	15
THÉN# .	16
you went on to the NÈXT topic#	17
(1.3:809–27)	

The tone units contain the following constituents, here ordered according to their rank in the syntactic hierarchy:

clause (simple sentence)	tone units 1, 2, 7, 17
nonfinite subclause	tone units 11, 12
divided clause	tone units 5+6, 8+10, 14+15
comment clause	tone unit 13
prepositional phrase	tone units 3, 4
word	tone units 16

The faked punctuation matches the prosodic division into tone units in four cases: full stop and end of tone unit 1, comma and end of tone units 6, 11 and 12. This emphasizes that there is very little agreement between (complex) sentences and tone units. On the other hand, the tone unit boundaries come between major constituents rather than single words, notably clauses and clause partials. The segmentation of the talk into tone units reflects the division of the message into information units, which in turn has an effect on the syntactic division.

▶▶▶▶▶ **Now try this!**

How would you chunk this piece of talk into:

    [a] tone units
    [b] grammatical units
    A: you can get all sorts of things there bought the aerial there but I went down a couple of weeks later when it still wasn't satisfactory and I asked for I said I priced |ði:| cable I said I wanted some coaxial cable as you know what I've been using on the old TV thing cos I was suspicious I've still got a hope that that what's wrong because you know it was in when we got this house that that |tə| television cable and of course the outside sheath really got bared a lot (1.7:797–813)

It may help you to know that it consists of 14 tone units in the original transcript.

[Suggested answer on pp 218–19]

Discourse units

The discourse level is the level beyond the sentence. There is consequently no need to anticipate a one-to-one correspondence between discourse units and syntactic units. Yet, as the following dialogue will show, the correspondence can be fairly high.

Moves and acts

In the following extract from a two-party dialogue the discourse structure in terms of moves and acts has been compared with the syntactic structure of each person's turn. In addition, the extent to which discourse and syntactic units agree with tone units has been examined.

Three types of move are represented, [Initiate] I, [Response] R, and [Follow-up] F. Each one of these is realized by one or more acts. The acts appear in the 'Discourse' column below, and the corresponding syntactic units in the 'Syntax' column. 'D' (in bold) stands for both interactional signals and discourse markers. The triple agreement between discourse, syntax and tone units is marked by an asterisk under 'TU':

[396]		Discourse	Syntax	TU
A: have you ever heard Professor Mc CÀLL LÉCTURE#	I	\<question\>	clause	★
he's round at TÒPAS		\<clue\>	clause	
I THÍNK#		**\<hedge\>**	**D**	
B: ★(NÓ))#★	R	**\<answer\>**	**D**	
A: ★I★ only ever went ÔNCE# .	I	\<inform\>	clause	★
it was ENÓUGH# –		\<expand\>	clause	★
B: M# – –	F	**\<acknowledge\>**	**D**	
A: **oh D ÊAR#**	I	**\<exclaim\>**	**D**	
Bridget will tell you THÁT# she was at the same LÈCTURE#		\<inform\> \<expand\>	clause clause	★ ★
B: M# – –	F	**\<acknowledge\>**	**D**	
what's he LÌKE#	I	\<question\>	clause	★
A: **oh**	R	**\<starter\>**	**D**	
he was TÊRRIBLE#		\<answer\>	clause	★
so ABSTRÚSE#		\<expand\>	clause	★
he does SÒUND changes#		\<expand\>	clause	★
and all THÁT SORT OF THING#		**\<filler\>**	**D**	
you KNÓW#		**\<empathizer\>**	**D**	
B: (– – – laughs) (1.6:894–912)	F	(laughter)		

The correspondence between discourse act, clause and tone unit is almost complete. The two exceptions, one involving a discourse marker *I THÍNK* the other an interactional signal *oh*. The \<expand\> *so ABSTRÚSE#* is an ellipted clause equivalent to 'he was so abstruse'.

One or more acts make up a move, and since an act usually corresponds to a clause and moves often consist of more than one act, it follows that the correspondence between moves and clauses is not overwhelming. In [396], the first [Initiate], for instance, corresponds to three clauses, since it is made up of three acts

(<question>, <clue>, <hedge>), each of which corresponds to a clause.

Notice that all the signals and markers, except *oh*, are pronounced in a separate tone unit.

Interactional signals and discourse markers

All through this book it has been obvious that, when people talk, they use a set of extremely frequent (single- and multi-word) items to start, carry on, and terminate a conversation. Some of these items constitute turns of their own, others link turns together, while still others serve as <stallers>, <frames> and <empathizers> within turns and, as has become apparent, many of them can do more than one thing in the discourse. Consider a particularly loaded example:

> [397] B: – *but* as I SÀY# I was ÒFFERED# a . a very
> PLÙM job# – ((*but* ə:)) . I feel if I stay at it here
> NÒW# I'll be here till I'm SIXTY-FÌVE# and I'll
> never get AWÀY# – *so* ə: –
> A: ((YÈAH)) I SUPPÓSE# if you got experience in
> American . university ADMINISTRÁTION# you
> could still come BÀCK# *here*
> B: *m* ÒH yes# . CÈRTAINLY# ((**well**)) they're
> desperate . for people to work in UNIVÉRSITIES#
> cos the MÓNEY'S not good# *– so* anyone*
> A: *oh RÉALLY# . ((**well you know**))* *oh* HÈRE
> {YÈAH#}# *m*
> B: *so* anybody who's soft enough to ENJÓY it#
> and *sort* of *ac*tually want a JÒB# **you**
> **KNÓW**# is *wel*comed with open
> A: *YÈS#* *YÈS#* *m#*
> >B: ÀRMS#
> A: YÈAH# . |s| – – – ṁ# – – – YÈS# **well** it'll be
> interesting to see how it WÒRKS# (1.5:1102–27)

Clearly, this is a very mixed lot but let us try to identify the items according to recent grammatical norms. We recognize the italicized items, which serve as links within and between the turns, as conjunctions (*and, but, cos*) and conjuncts (*so*). The items printed in bold, which are used as <frames>, <stallers> and

<empathizers>, consist of a disjunct (*actually*), a subjunct (*sort of*), an adverbial particle (*well*) and a comment clause (*you know*). The underlined items, which serve as [responses] and feedback signals, consist of an interjection (*oh*) and reaction signals (*m*, *really*, *yeah*, *yes*). But is this a purely grammatical description? The answer is 'no'. The borderline between grammar in the traditional sense and discourse analysis is fuzzy indeed.

What makes this type of items particularly difficult to classify is not only the fact that they often do more than one thing at once and work at more than one level but also the fact that the same function can be realized by more than one of them. *Yes*, *really* and *certainly*, for instance, can all be used as [responses].

The majority of the items concerned, can be divided into the following categories:

ONLY INTERACTIONAL	lexical items that cannot be described as clause elements
MAINLY INTERACTIONAL	lexical items primarily used as interactional devices but also used as clause elements
ALSO INTERACTIONAL	adverbials used as interactional or discourse-organizing devices

ONLY INTERACTIONAL	MAINLY INTERACTIONAL	ALSO INTERACTIONAL
ah	alright	absolutely
aha	I mean	actually
mhm	I see	anyway
oh	no	certainly
yeah	OK	honestly
yes	please	however
	right	indeed
	sure	in fact
	tags	matbe
	thank you	now
	that's alright	obviously
	that's right	of course
	well	perhaps
	you know	probably
	you see	really

Finally, the three categories can be seen along a **clause-integration** scale, which shows that the more interactional an item is the less integrated it is in the clause and vice versa:

Pure	**+ interaction**	**+ integration**	Clause
inter-	----------------------------------		function
action	**− integration**	**− interaction**	

Conclusion

We can safely conclude from this brief survey that interactional signals and discourse markers are better described in pragmatic than in grammatical terms. Other talk, on the other hand, can fairly easily be taken care of within the area of grammar.

▶▶▶▶ **Now try this!**

At this stage, it should be possible for you to apply the entire system of analysis described in this book to a piece of conversation. The extract is from a conversation between two teachers, one female and one male, who are talking about certain colleagues (some slight modifications have been made):

[a] outline the topical framework
[b] give a detailed analysis in terms of transaction, exchanges, turns, moves and acts

A: did you arrange to have LÚNCH with Jamie#
B: no I DÌDN'T#
A: NÓ#
B: NÒ#
   I I just sort of said – let's SÒMETIME# or SÒMETHING
   VÁGUE# you KNÓW# bit SÍLLY#
A: *YÈAH#*
B: but əm – YÈAH# – oh I must DÒ that SÓMETIME# –
   oh YÈS# ÓNE thing# TÒO# . ə:m . are you at all
   interested in coming to the B minor MÁSS# –
A: WHÉN is it# the fifteenth of ÁPRIL#
B: YÈAH# –
A: əm – when ÌS that# . *NÈXT week#*
B: *that's next* TÙESDAY# – – .
A: I'll ask Trish TONÌGHT#
   I think . it's the day before she goes back to SCHÒOL#

B: M̀#
A: and – she may be DÓING something#
B: YÈAH#
A: if she . if she would like to CÓME# Ì will come#
B: MH́M# – (* –* – giggles)
A: *where*
B: in other WÓRDS# you'll CÓME if your GÌRLFRIEND
   wants to come#
A: YÈS# (7.3:653:66)

[Suggested answer on pp 219–20]

If you want to know more:

on aspects of speech and writing, see Biber (1988), Brown and Yule
(1983) Ch.1, Chafe (1982), Fox (1987), Halliday (1989), Tannen
(ed) (1984);
on discourse and grammar, see Geluykens (1992), Goodwin (1979),
Green (1989) Ch.6, Halliday (1989), Ch.6, Hopper (1982), James
(1972, 1978), Reichman (1981), Stenström (1986, 1987, 1989,
1990c).

Answers to the exercises

▶▶▶▶▶ p 34

[b] consists of four exchanges:

B: how did you get on with CHÀUCER# . ⎤
A: WÈLL# I LÍKED it# ⎦ Exchange 1

B: you LÌKED it# ⎤
do you REMÉMBER any Chaucer
{NÓW}#} – ⎬ Exchange 2
A: ə:m . ⎦

B: what did you RÈAD# . you read |ði:| ⎤
PRÓLOGUE#
the TÀLES# ⎬ Exchange 3
A: the PRÓLOGUE# {YÈS#}# ⎦

B: well . did you read any of the TÁLES# ⎤
A: YÈS# the PÀRDONER# ⎥
B: The PÁRDONER'S# The Nun's Prist's ⎬ Exchange 4
TÀLE# ⎥
A: YÈS# ⎦

▶▶▶▶▶ p 38

(a) A and B make one move each, an [Initiate] and a
[Response].
(b) Both moves are complex. A's [Initiate] consists of three
acts; B's [Response] consists of two acts.

▶▶▶▶▶ p 43

A: I don't think you've BÈEN upstairs YÉT#   <question>
B: only just to the LÒO#   <answer>
A: YÈAH# –   <acknowledge>

ə: well . Sidney HÈATH {sort of
lives UPSTÀIRS#}#   <inform>
B: *Y=ES#* =M#   <acknowledge>
A: but he's really seems to work more
with . HÁRT#   <inform>
B: YÈAH#   <agree>

▶▶▶▶▶ p 46

[a] we've got to do a grand TÒUR#   <expand>
[b] and grotesque as they may BÊ# they .   <expand>
capture some ÀSPECTS of REÁLITY#
YÈS#   <emphasizer>

▶▶▶▶▶ p 48

The three complementary acts are:

the <monitor> *I mean*
the <hedge> *sort of*
the <empathizer> *you know*

▶▶▶▶▶ p 55

The two exchanges represent the following patterns:

A: q1 do you and your husband have
            a CÁR#
B: q2 have a CÀR#
A: a2 YÈAH#   Exchange 1
B: a1 NÒ#
A: F   ÒH#

B: q1 how do you move ABÒUT#
        a1 by tube or a BÙS or whatever# .   Exchange 2
            you KNÒW#
A: F   how very PLEBÈIAN#

A [Follow-up<acknowledge>] terminates the first exchange
and
a [Follow-up<evaluate>] terminates the second exchange.

▶▶▶▶▶ p 57

I = [Initiate]; R = [Response]; F = [Follow-up]

A: ə:m do you and your husband have a
    CÁR#   [I<question>]
B: have a CÁR#   [Repair<question>]
A: YÉAH#   [R<confirm>]
B: NÒ#   [R<answer>]
A: ÒH#.   [F<acknowledge>]
    how do you move ABÒUT#   [I<question>]
B: by tube or a BÙS or whatever# .   [R<answer>
    you KNÓW#   <empathizer>]
A: how very PLEBÈIAN# – –   [F<evaluate>]

▶▶▶▶▶ p 58

[a]
A: has Ivor gone HÓME# –   [I<question>]
B: I THÍNK so#   [R<answer>]
A: has the sixth form conference FÌNISHED
    then#   [I<question>]
B: YÈS   [R<answer>
    well# .   <monitor>
    it finished really last NÌGHT#   <expand>]

[b] the exchange pattern is 'chaining'

▶▶▶▶▶ p 62

R = [Response]; B = [Backchannel]; F = [Follow-up]

NÓ   = [R<answer>]
UHÙH   = [B<acknowledge>]
M̀   = [F<accept>]
ÒK RÍGHT   = [R<accept><emphasizer>]
ÒK   = [I<call-off>]
GRÈAT YÉAH   = [R<close>]
all RÍGHT   = [I<call-off>]
RÌGHT   = [R<close>]
(WÈLL is a discourse marker)

▶▶▶▶▶ p 66

This is how the markers appeared in the original:

A: I find it rather DÌFFICULT# to assess **you see . in a**
    ẂAY# Eileen has moved into a very **sort of** – rather
    ÒUTBACK **kind of** PLÁCE# – and as a RESÚLT# she
    doesn't – – – expect perhaps – – the **kind of** – –

SUCCÈSSES {I SUPPÓSE that#}# – – **I mean** when we lived in the PÓTTERIES# in our YÓUTH# – even to know ÀNYBODY who wrote a BÓOK# was quite SÓMETHING . **WÀSN'T it**#

▶▶▶▶▶ p 83

[a] Turntaking: filled pause ə (line 1)
interruption ⋆*well one's AWÁRE*⋆ . . . (line 13)

[b] Turnholding: strategically placed silent pause, *you can't hold – – the top administrative job* (line 1)
filled pause *that ə DEGRÈE* (line 9)

[c] Turnyielding: empathizer *you KNÓW* (lines 5, 6); falling tone + brief pause (line 7)

▶▶▶▶▶ p 87

[a] by the <starter> *well* followed by the <frame> NÓW
[b] by the <preface> *what about THÍS*
[c] by the [summons] *CHÁIRMAN* followed by the <meta-statement> *may I raise a completely DÍFFERENT point*

▶▶▶▶▶ p 92

The first half of the utterance is an <inform>, ie presents 'neutral' information; the second half is an <opine>, ie shows the speaker's attitude.

▶▶▶▶▶ p 102

[a]   **most polite**

1   I wonder if you could put me on your MÁILING-LIST please
2   is she THÉRE please
3   would you TÉLL him
4   could you give her a MÉSSAGE for me
5   can you ÀSK her to ring her SOLÍCITORS
6   will you pass that ÓN to him#
7   do you KNÓW the ADDRÈSS
8   how about somebody giving MÈ a game

                                         least polite

[b] What complicates matters most of all is of course that the <requests> are out of context.

▶▶▶▶ p 103

[a] Despite its declarative form, *I'm not just WÀSTING my TÍME* functions as a <question>. In other words, it is the second part of the utterance that is answered;

[b] *how many people have STÀYED with us* is a rhetorical question. Despite the interrogative form, it functions as a forceful statement; a possible paraphrase would be 'we've had such a lot of people staying with us already'.

▶▶▶▶ pp 108–9

A: [well I PREFÈR# Lord of the FLÌES# – –
B: [(R)/Q WHỲ#

A: [A because I don't think I UNDERSTÒOD Pincher MÁRTIN# .

The [R<reply>] to A's [I<inform> is ellipted; *oh* or *do you* can be implied.

▶▶▶▶ p 113

Both [responses] indicate 'information received', but they do it differently. The first M̆, with a falling-rising tone, reflects a certain degree of interest and encourages A to go on, while =M, with a level tone, just endorses what was said.

▶▶▶▶ pp 115–16

[a] a <supply> (or possibly an <evade>)
[b] A: has Ivor gone HÓME#   yes/no   <comply>
    he had to do
        his homework <imply>
    none of my
        problems   <evade>
    I've no idea   <disclaim>

▶▶▶▶ p 117

ÓK, ÒK and CÉRTAINLY could answer <permission requests>

▶▶▶▶ p 120

A: have a glass of SHÉRRY I'd love one thank
                                you   <accept>
                        I'm a bit pressed for
                                time   <evade>
                        sorry I'm driving   <reject>

▶▶▶▶ p 121

I'm SÒRRY (polite but noncommittal)
SÓRRY (asking for repetition or clarification)
I'm SǑRRY (polite and apologetic)

▶▶▶▶ p 122

You could say, for instance: 'my pleasure'

▶▶▶▶ p 124

What A said in the original version was simply: NÓ.

▶▶▶▶ p 126

What A said in the original version was: *oh this AFTERNÒON#*
SǑRRY# . SǑRRY#

▶▶▶▶ pp 132–3

[a]
well   <starter>
I mean   <monitor>
ÒBVIOUSLY   <emphasizer>
I mean   <monitor>
RÉALLY   <filler> (or <emphasizer>)
ə:m ə   <staller>

[b]
sort of   <hedge> with *quite . quite* intensifying
you see   <empathizer>
you know   <empathizer>
HÁVEN'T you   <appealer>

▶▶▶▶ p 148

[a] home – individual – self
[b] work – secretary – self
[c] home/work – individual
[d] telephonist-> individual

▶▶▶▶▶ p 162

SÒ# *there we* ÀRE definitely terminates the old topic. But it also serves as a transition to a new topic, although it does not really introduce anything.

▶▶▶▶▶ p 166

[b] and [d] are telephone closings;
[a] is from a conversation between two male teachers at work;
[c] is from a conversation between a former employer and a former employee;

▶▶▶▶ pp 168–9

a: hello Ann it's Joan B: HELLÒ {JÒAN#}#	] greeting	⎤
a: (sings Happy Birthday) B: THÁNK you#	] congratu- lation	OPENING
I DÌD have {a nice BÍRTHDAY#}# ...	]	] MESSAGE
B: all RÍGHT# – – ... a: ...*out*side the dome	⎤ pre-closing	⎤
B: *OK̗#* – *RÌGHT#* a: *OK* then	] closing	CLOSING
B: bye BỲE# a: bye bye	] farewell	⎦

▶▶▶▶▶ p 181

A narrowing–down–to–essentials technique, which leads stepwise to a 'conclusion'. Notice that the <questions> are realized by declaratives (once with a tag) and are more like <statements>.

▶▶▶▶ p 189

It is more formal. The person who wishes to take the floor turns to the chairman and asks permission to speak instead of just barging in, as in the committee meeting. The main difference from the radio discussion is that the speaker self-selects instead of being selected.

▶▶▶▶ pp 197–8

* the choice of vocabulary (*frightfully posh*, *livened ÙP TÈRRIBLY*, *you don't half look STÚPID*;
* the use of \<appealers\> (*ÌSN'T it*, *ÌS it*;
* the use of \<boosters\> (*CÒR*).
* the many instances of simultaneous speech

▶▶▶▶ p 205

[a] This is how the original conversation was analysed into tone units:

A: you can get all SÒRTS of things THÉRE# .
bought the ÁERIAL THÉRE# –
but I went down a couple of weeks LÁTER#
when it still wasn't SATISFÁCTORY# .
and I asked for |ə| . I . said . I PRÍCED#
|ði:| CÀBLE#
I said I wanted some coaxial CÀBLE as# .
YǑU know#
what I've . been using on the old TǓ thing# –
cos I was SUSPǏCIOUS#
I've still got a hope that that's what's WRÒNG#
because YǑU know#
it was in when we got this HÒUSE#
that that |tə| TELEVÌSION cable#

[b] And this is one way of chunking the extract into grammatical units:
You can get all sorts of things there.
Bought the aerial there.
But I went down a couple of weeks later, when it still wasn't satisfactory, and I asked for – I said I priced the cable.
I said I wanted some coaxial cable, you know, what I've been using on the old TV thing, cos I was suspicious.

I've still got a hope that that's what's wrong, because, you know, it was in when we got this house that television cable.

We end up with five sentences. This is not surprising, considering that a tone unit is more likely to contain a clause, or a phrase, than a sentence.

▶▶▶▶ pp 209–10

[a] Two topics are discussed: 'the lunch with Jamie' and 'coming to the B minor mass', which means that this piece of conversation consists of two transactions. The <frame> *oh* YÈS and the <preface> ÓNE *thing* TÒO serve as transition markers between the two transactions.

[b]

A: did you arrange to have LÚNCH   [I<question>]
    with Jamie#

B: no I DÌDN'T#   [R<answer]

A: NÒ#   [Re-open<query>]

B: NÒ#   [R<confirm>
    I I just sort of said – let's   <expand>+<hedge>
    SÒMETIME#   +<empathizer>
    or SÓMETHING *VÁGUE#* you
    KNÓW# bit SÍLLY# –

A: *YÈAH#*   [B<acknowledge>]

B: but əm – YÈAH# – oh I must   <frame><expand>]
    DÒ that SÓMETIME# –
    oh YÈS# ÓNE **thing**#   [Focus<frame><preface>]
    TÒO# .
    ə:m . are you at all interested in   <question>
    coming
    to the B minor MÁSS# –

A: WHÉN is it# the fifteenth   [Repair<check>+<clue>]
    of ÁPRIL#

B: YÈAH# –   [R<confirm>]

A: əm – when ÌS that# .   [Repair<check>+<clue>]
    NÈXT week#

B: *that's next* TÙESDAY# – – .   [R<confirm>]

A: I'll ask Trish TONÍGHT#   [R<supply>
    I think . it's the day before she goes   <expand>
    back to SCHÒOL#

B: M̀#   [B<acknowledge>]

A: and – she may be DÒING something#   <expand>]

B: YÈAH#   [F<acknowledge>]

A: if she . if she would like to CÓME#   <answer>]
   Ì will come#

B: MH̀M# – (*–* – – giggles)   [F<acknowledge>]

A: *where*

B: in other WÒRDS# you'll CÓME if your [I<suggest>]
   GÌRLFRIEND
   wants to come#

A: YÈS#   [R<answer>]

Glossary

\<accept\>	signals acceptance
\<acknowledge\>	signals receipt of information
act	the lowest rank in the hierarchy, signalling the speaker's intention
\<action request\>	asks somebody to do something
adjacency pair	consists of two consecutive and closely linked acts, eg \<question\>-\<answer\>
\<agree\>	signals agreement
\<alert\>	calls somebody's attention
anaphoric reference	refers to something already mentioned
\<answer\>	responds to a \<question\>
\<apology\>	expresses regret
\<appealer\>	invites feedback
aside	comment outside the conversation proper
B-event	something that is known only to B
[backchannel]	signals listener attention
\<booster\>	the speaker's assessment of what s/he says
\<call-off\>	prompts the closing of a conversation
chaining	type of exchange pattern
\<check\>	asks for clarification or repetition
\<closer\>	ends the closing of a conversation
closing	post-message talk ending the conversation
\<clue\>	gives a hint
coherent	what is said hangs together and makes sense

cohesive	what is said is linguistically linked
complementary act	accompanies primary/secondary act
\<comply\>	answers a \<question\> directly
\<confirm\>	responds to a \<confirmation question\>
\<confirmation question\>	asks for confirmation
context	any background information related to a conversation
conventional implicature	meaning implicit in an utterance whose form does not match its meaning but which is conventionally taken to have that specific meaning
conversational implicature	an implied meaning which can be derived in a rational way from an utterance although it is not expressed
cooperative principle	according to Grice, a general rule governing conversation
coupling	type of exchange pattern
covert	implicit
digression	temporary break-off from a topic
\<disagree\>	expresses disagreement
\<disclaim\>	expresses 'I don't know'
discourse act	the pragmatic content of what is uttered
discourse marker	organizes the conversation
distant speakers	speakers who don't know each other well
echo question	a question which repeats part or all of the preceding utterance and expresses strong surprise or emphasis
elliptical coupling	type of exchange pattern
embedding	type of exchange pattern
\<empathizer\>	'involves' the listener
\<emphasizer\>	acts as a reinforcer
\<evade\>	avoids answering
\<evaluate\>	assesses what the previous speaker said
exchange	the smallest interactive unit

exophoric reference	refers to the extra-linguistic situation
<expand>	gives complementary information
expletive	strong word, swear-word
feedback	any listener reaction to what the speaker has said
<filler>	lexically empty item with uncertain discourse functions, except to fill a conversational gap
[focus]	introduces an [initiate]
[follow-up]	terminates an exchange
<frame>	marks a boundary in the discourse
gap filler	fills a gap in the exchange
<greeting>	greets somebody
<hedge>	modifies what is being said by reducing its force
<identification question>	asks for the identifiction of a *wh*-word
<imply>	answers a <question> indirectly
implicature	see under **conventional implicature** and **conversational implicature**
inference	conclusion drawn from what has been said
<inform>	provides objective information
information unit	the amount of information given in a tone unit
[initiate]	opens an exchange
intended implicature	what the speaker means without saying it plainly
intended meaning	what the speaker means
interactional signal	item that helps us interact
interactional strategies	strategies adopted to carry on a conversation and achieve a purpose
interactive linking	eg what ties <question> and <answer> together
intimate speakers	speakers who know each other well
<invite>	asks if somebody would like to do something

<justify>	defends what was said in a previous act
link	connects sentences, clauses and turns
literal meaning	word-by-word 'face-value' meaning
message	what the conversation is about
<metacomment>	a comment on current talk
<monitor>	a device that helps the speaker put things right
move	what the speaker does in order to interact
non–surreptitious speaker	speaker who is aware of being recorded
nucleus	the most prominent syllable in a tone unit
<object>	signals a different opinion
<offer>	presents something for acceptance
opening	pre-message talk
<opine>	expresses personal opinion
overt	explicit
pause unit	what is said between two pauses
perceived implicature	B's interpretation of what A said
perceived meaning	what B thinks that A means
performance unit	the content of a pause unit
<permission request>	asks permission to do something
phatic talk	warming-up and winding-up talk
pitch	intonation contour
pitch–prominent	carrying the nuclear tone
<polarity question>	asks for a *yes/no* <answer>
pragmatic meaning	meaning in context
pragmatic strategies	strategies in context
<precursor>	introduces a <question>
<preface>	introduces a primary act
primary act	the only obligatory act in a move
principle of end focus	rule saying that the most important information comes at the end
principle of relevance	according to Sperber and Wilson (1986): 'Every act of inferential communication creates a presumption of optimal relevance'
prompt	urge something to happen

prosodic linking	the effect of A's [response]-inviting pitch contour on B's [response]
Q-tag	*isn't it, hasn't he* etc
<query>	expresses doubt and surprise
<question>	asks for information, confirmation, clarification
<react>	expresses B's attitude to what A said
<reject>	expresses disagreement
[re-opener]	delays the termination of an exchange
[repair]	holds up the exchange for explanatory reasons
<reply>	responds to a <statement>/<request>
<request>	asks somebody to do something
[response]	continues or terminates an exchange
response marker	initiates a response
resumption marker	initiates a topic resumption
secondary act	accompanies a primary act
shared knowledge	knowledge that A and B have in common
slot filler	fills a slot in the turn
<smoother>	responds to an <apology>
smooth speaker shift	A finishes before B takes over
speech act	what the speaker 'does' by saying something
speech-in-action	extra-topical talk embedded in the conversation
speech situation	time and place of conversation, topic and speakers involved
<staller>	plays for time
<starter>	helps getting started
<statement>	supplies 'information'
subordinate tone unit	with a pitch-range falling within the pitch-range of a main tone unit
subtopic	an aspect of a main topic
<suggest>	puts forward an idea
[summons]	opens a conversation by calling the listener's attention

\<supply\>	answers beside the point
surreptitious speaker	speaker who does not know that s/he is being recorded
\<thanks\>	express gratitude
tone unit	word group containing a nucleus
tone unit boundary	marks beginning and end of tone unit
tonicity	placement of the nuclear tone
topic	the subject for conversation
topic-boundary	boundary between topics/sub-topics
topic-boundary marker	marks topic transitions
topic change	a move to a completely new topic
topic drift	an inconspicuous shift of topics
topic resumption	going back after a digression
topic shift	a move to a related topic
transaction	the highest unit in the hierarchy, dealing with one topic
turn	everything the current speaker says 'at one go'
unsmooth speaker shift	B takes over before A has finished
unit pause	the standard-length pause
\<uptake\>	accepts what was said and leads on
utterance	anything that a speaker says

References

Adler, M. (1978) *Naming and addressing: A sociolinguistic study*. Hamburg: Helmut Buske.

Aijmer, K. (1984) *Sort of* and *kind of* in English conversation. *Studia Linguistica* **38**, 118–128.

Aijmer, K. (1986) Why is *actually* so frequent in spoken English? In G. Tottie and I. Bäcklund (eds) (1986) 119–129.

Aijmer, K. (1987) *Oh* and *ah* in English conversation. In W. Meijs (ed.) (1987), 61–86.

Altenberg, B. (1987) *Prosodic patterns in spoken English*. Lund: Lund University Press.

Atkinson, M. (1984) *Our masters' voices*. London: Methuen.

Atkinson, J. and P. Drew. (1979) *Order in court*. London: Macmillan.

Atkinson, J. and J. Heritage (eds) (1984) *Structures of social action*. Cambridge: Cambridge University Press.

Austin, J. (1962) *How to do things with words*. Oxford: Oxford University Press.

Bailey, R. (1985) Negotiations and meaning: revisiting the context of situation. In J. Benson and W. Greaves (eds) *Systemic perspectives on discourse*, vol. 2. New Jersey: Ablex.

Beattie, G. (1981) The regulation of speaker turns in face-to-face conversation: some implications for conversation in sound-only channels. *Semiotica* **34**, 55–70.

Bennett, A. (1981) Interruptions and the interpretation of conversation. *Discourse processes* **4**, 171–188.

Biber, D. (1988) *Variation across speech and writing*. Cambridge: Cambridge University Press.

Blum-Kulka, S. (1987) Indirectness and politeness in requests: same or different? *Journal of Pragmatics* **11**, 131–146.

Brazil, D. (1985) *The communicative value of intonation in English*.

Birmingham: English language research, University of Birmingham.

Brown, G. (1977) *Listening to spoken English*. London: Longman.

Brown, G. (1983) Prosodic structure and the given/new distinction. In A. Cutler and R. Ladd (eds) *Prosody: Models and Methods*. Berlin: Springer-Verlag.

Brown, G., Currie, K. and J. Kenworthy. (1980) *Questions of intonation*. London: Croom-Helm.

Brown, G. and G. Yule. (1983) *Discourse analysis*. Cambridge: Cambridge University Press.

Brown, P. and S. Levinson. (1978) Universals in language use: politeness phenomena. In E. Goody (ed.) *Questions and politeness: Strategies in social interaction*. Cambridge: Cambridge University Press.

Bublitz, W. (1988) *Supportive fellow-speakers and cooperative conversations*. Amsterdam: John Benjamins.

Burton, D. (1980) *Dialogue and discourse*. London: Routledge & Kegan Paul.

Button, G. and N. Casey. (1985) Topic nomination and topic pursuit. *Human Studies* **8**, 3–55.

Button, G. and J. Lee (eds) (1987) *Talk and social organisation*. Clevedon, England: Multilingual Matters.

Chafe, W. (1982) Integration and involvement in speaking, writing, and oral literature. In D. Tannen (ed.) *Spoken and written language: Exploring orality and literacy*. New Jersey: Ablex.

Cheepen, C. (1988) *The predictability of informal conversation*. London: Pinter Publishers.

Cheepen, C. and J. Monaghan. (1990) *Spoken English. A practical guide*. London: Pinter Publishers.

Coulmas, E. (ed) (1981) *Conversational Routine*. The Hague: Mouton.

Coulthard, M. (1977) *An introduction to discourse analysis*. London: Longman.

Coulthard, M. and M. Montgomery (eds) (1981) *Studies in discourse analysis*. London: Routledge and Kegan Paul.

Craig, R. and K. Tracy (eds) (1983) *Conversational coherence: form, structure and strategy*. London: Sage Publications.

Crow, B. (1983) Topic shifts in couples' conversations. In R. Craig and K. Tracey (eds) *Conversational coherence*. London: Sage Publications.

Crystal, D. (1969) *Prosodic systems and intonation in English*. Cambridge: Cambridge University Press.

Crystal, D. and D. Davy. (1975) *Advanced conversational English.* London: Longman.

Cutler, A. and M. Pearson (1986) On the analysis of prosodic turn-taking cues. In C. Johns-Lewis (ed.) *Intonation in Discourse.* London: Croom-Helm.

Edmondson, W. (1981) *Spoken discourse: A model for analysis.* London: Longman.

Ellis, R. and A. McClintock (1990) *If you take my meaning.* London: Edward Arnold.

Erman, B. (1987) *Pragmatic expressions in English: A study of 'you know', 'you see', and 'I mean' in face-to-face conversation.* Stockholm: Almqvist & Wiksell.

Fairclough, N. (1989) *Language and power.* London: Longman.

Fox, B. (1987) *Discourse structure and anaphora.* Cambridge: Cambridge University Press.

Geluykens, R. (1988) On the myth of rising intonation in polar questions. *Journal of Pragmatics* **12**, 467–485.

Geluykens, R. (1992) *From discourse process to grammatical construction.* Amsterdam: John Benjamins.

Gibbs, R. (1987) Mutual knowledge and the psychology of conversational inference. *Journal of Pragmatics* **11**, 561–588.

Goffman, E. (1967) *Interaction ritual: essays in face-to-face behaviour.* Chicago: Aldine Publishing Co.

Goffman, E. (1976) Replies and responses. *Language in Society* **5**, 257–313.

Goffman, E. (1978) Response cries. *Language* **54**, 787–815.

Goffman, E. (1979) *Forms of talk.* Oxford: Blackwell.

Goodrich, P. (1987) *Legal discourse: studies in linguistic, rhetoric and legal analysis.* London: Macmillan.

Goodwin, C. (1979) The interactive construction of a sentence in natural conversation. In G. Psathas (ed.) *Everyday language.* New York: John Wiley.

Goodwin, C. (1981) *Conversational organization: Interactions between speakers and hearers.* New York: Academic Press.

Green, G. (1989) *Pragmatics and natural language understanding.* Hillsdale, New Jersey: Lawrence Erlbaum.

Grice, H. (1975) Logic and conversation. In P. Cole and J. Morgan (eds) *Syntacs and semantics.* Vol 3. New York: Academic Press.

Grimes, J.(1975) *The thread of discourse.* The Hague: Mouton.

Gumperz. J. (1982) *Discourse strategies.* Cambridge: Cambridge University Press.

Halliday, M.A.K. (1989) *Spoken and written language*. Oxford: Oxford University Press.

Halliday, M.A.K. and R. Hasan (1976) *Cohesion in English*. London: Longman.

Heritage, J. (1984) A change-of-state token and aspects of its sequential placement. In J. Atkinson and J. Heritage (eds) (1984) 299–345.

Hopper, P. (1982) Aspect between discourse and grammar. In P. Hopper (ed.) *Tense-aspect: Between semantics and pragmatics*. Amsterdam: John Benjamins.

Hopper, P. (1989) Speech in telephone openings: Emergent interaction v. routines. *Western Journal of Speech Communication* **53**, 178–194.

James, D. (1972) Some aspects of the syntax and semantics of interjections. *Papers from the 8th regional meeting, Chicago linguistic society*, 162–172) Chicago: Linguistics department, University of Chicago.

James, D. (1978) The use of *oh, ah, say* and *well* in relation to a number of grammatical phenomena. *Papers in Linguistics* **11**, 517–535.

Jefferson, G. (1972) Side sequences. In D. Sudnow (ed.)(1972) *Studies in social interaction*, 294–388. New York: The Free Press.

Jefferson, G. (1987) On exposed and embedded correction in conversation. In G. Button and J. Lee (eds) *Talk and social organisation of conversational interaction*, 219–248. Clevedon, England: Multilingual Matters.

Labov, W. and D. Fanshel (1977) *Therapeutic discourse*. New York: Academic Press.

Leech, G. (1980) Language and tact. In *Explorations in Semantics & Pragmatics*, 79–117.

Leech, G. (1983) *Principles of pragmatics*. London: Longman.

Levinson, S. (1983) *Pragmatics*. Cambridge: Cambridge University Press.

Mandelbaum, J. (1979) Interpersonal activities in conversational storytelling. *Western Journal of Speech Communication*, **53**, 114–126.

McCarthy, M. (1991) *Discourse analysis for language teachers*. Cambridge: Cambridge University Press.

McLaughlin, M. (1984) *Conversation. How talk is organized*. Beverly Hills, Ca.: Sage Publications.

McTear, M.F. (1979) Is conversation structured?: towards an analysis of informal spoken discourse. In W. Wolck and P.

Garvin (eds) (1979) *The Fifth Lacus Forum* (1977) Columbia SC: Hornbeam Press.

Meijs, W. (ed.) (1987) *Corpus linguistics and beyond*. Amsterdam: Rodopi.

Merritt, M. (1976) On questions following questions in service encounters. *Language in Society* **5**, 315–357.

Monaghan, J. (ed.) (1987) *Grammar in the construction of texts*. London: Frances Pinter.

Nofsinger, R. (1991) *Everyday conversation*. London: Sage Publications.

Oreström, B. (1983) *Turn-taking in English conversation*. Lund: Lund University Press.

Östman, J-O. (1981) *You know. A discourse-functional approach*. Amsterdam: John Benjamins.

Quirk, R., Greenbaum, S., Leech, G. and J. Svartvik (1985) *A comprehensive grammar of the English language*. London: Longman.

Reichman, R. (1981) *Plain speaking: a theory of grammar of spontaneous discourse*. Cambridge, Mass.: Bolt, Beranek and Newman, report 4681.

Richards, J. and R. Schmidt (eds) (1983) *Language and communication*. London: Longman.

Roger, D. and P. Bull. (eds) (1988) *Conversation*. Clevedon, Philadelphia: Multilingual Matters.

Sacks, H., Schegloff, E. and G. Jefferson (1974) A simplest systematics for the organisation of turn-taking for conversation. *Language* **50** (4), 696–735.

Schegloff, E. (1968) Sequencing in conversational openings. In J. Gumperz and D. Hymes (eds) *Directions in sociolinguistics*. New York: Rinehart & Winston.

Schegloff, E. (1982) Discourse as an interactional achievement: Some uses of 'uh huh' and other things that come between sentences. In D. Tannen (ed.) *Analysing discourse: Text and talk*. Washington DC: Georgetown University Press.

Schegloff, E. and H. Sacks (1973) Opening up closings. *Semiotica* **8** (4), 289–327.

Schegloff, E., Jefferson, G. and H. Sacks (1977) The preference for self-correction in the organization of repair in conversation. *Language* **53**, 361–382.

Schenkein, J. (ed) (1978) *Studies in the organization of conversational interaction*. New York: Academic Press.

Schiffrin, D. (1987) *Discourse markers*. Cambridge: Cambridge University Press.

Schourup, L. (1985) *Common discourse particles in English conversation: like, well, y'know.* New York: Garland.

Searle, J. (1969) *Speech acts: an essay in the philosophy of language.* Cambridge: Cambridge University Press.

Sinclair, J. and M. Coulthard (1975). *Towards an analysis of discourse: The English used by teachers and pupils.* Oxford: Oxford University Press.

Sperber, D. and D. Wilson (1986) *Relevance.* Oxford: Blackwell.

Stenström, A-B. (1984) *Questions and responses in English conversation.* Lund: Lund University Press.

Stenström, A-B. (1986) What does *really* really do? Strategies in speech and writing. In G. Tottie and I. Bäcklund (eds) (1986) 149–163. [Also in Monaghan, J. (ed.) (1987) 65–79.]

Stenström, A-B. (1987) Carry-on signals in English conversation. In W. Meijs (ed.) (1987) 87–120.

Stenström, A-B. (1988) Questioning in conversation. In M. Meyer (ed.) *Questions and questioning.* Berlin: de Gruyter.

Stenström, A-B. (1989) Discourse signals: Towards a model of analysis. In H. Weydt (ed.) *Sprechen mit Partikeln,* 561–574. Berlin: de Gruyter.

Stenström, A-B. (1990a) Lexical items peculiar to spoken discourse. In J. Svartvik (ed.) (1990) Ch. 5.

Stenström, A-B. (1990b) Pauses in monologue and dialogue. In J. Svartvik (ed.). (1990) Ch. 8.

Stenström, A-B. (1990c) Adverbial commas and prosodic segmentation. In J. Svartvik (ed) (1990) Ch. 9.

Stenström, A-B. (1991) Expletives in the London–Lund Corpus. In K. Aijmer and B. Altenberg (eds) *English corpus linguistics. Studies in honour of Jan Svartvik,* 239–253. London: Longman.

Stubbs, M. (1983) *Discourse analysis.* Oxford: Blackwell.

Svartvik, J. (1980) *Well* in conversation. In S. Greenbaum, G. Leech and J. Svartvik (eds) *Studies in English linguistics for Randolph Quirk.* London: Longman.

Svartvik, J. (ed.) (1990) *The London-Lund Corpus of spoken English: Description and research.* Lund: Lund University Press.

Svartvik, J. and R. Quirk. (eds) (1980) *A corpus of English conversation.* Lund: Lund University Press.

Tannen, D. (ed.) (1984) *Coherence in spoken and written discourse.* New Jersey: Ablex.

Tannen, D. (1986) *That's not what I meant.* New York: William Morrow.

Tannen, D. (1989) *Talking voices: Repetition, dialogue, and imagery in conversational discourse.* Cambridge: Cambridge University Press.

Tannen, D. (1990) *You just don't understand.* New York: William Morrow.

Taylor, T. and D. Cameron. (1987) *Analysing conversation.* Oxford: Pergamon Press.

Thavenius, C. (1983) *Referential pronouns in English conversation.* Lund: Lund University Press.

Thomas, J.A. (1985) The language of power: towards a dynamic pragmatics, *Journal of Pragmatics* **9**, 765–84.

Tomlin, R. (ed.) (forthcoming) *Coherence and grounding in discourse.* Amsterdam: John Benjamins.

Tottie, G. (1989) What does *uh-(h)uh* mean? In B. Odenstedt and G. Persson (eds). *Instead of flowers. Papers in honour of Mats Rydén on the occasion of his sixtieth birthday, August 27, 1989.* Stockholm: Almqvist & Wiksell.

Tottie, G. and I. Bäcklund (eds) (1986) *English in speech and writing: A symposium.* Stockholm: Almqvist & Wiksell.

Wardhaugh, R. (1985) *How conversation works.* Oxford: Blackwell.

Watts, R., Ide, S. and K. Ehlich (eds) (1992) *Politeness in language: Studies in its history, theory and practice.* Berlin: Mouton de Gruyter.

Wilson, J. (1990) *Politically speaking.* Oxford: Blackwell.

Index